Fear of Rejection

NLP Tools You Can Use

There are so many things in human living that we should regard not as traumatic learning but as incomplete learning, unfinished learning.

- Milton H. Erickson

Dedicated to the memory of

Prof. Jay Haley

Disclaimer

The information contained in this book is not intended to be a substitute for professional medical or mental health advice, diagnosis, or treatment. Always seek the advice of a qualified healthcare provider or mental health professional with any questions you may have regarding a medical or mental health condition.

The author makes no representation or warranties, express or implied. In no event shall the author, any contributors or editors, or anyone referenced as a source or authority be liable for any claims or damages (including, without limitation, direct, incidental and consequential damages, personal injury/wrongful death, lost profits, resulting from the use of or inability to use this book, whether based on warranty, contract, tort, or any other legal theory, and whether or not the author is advised of the possibility of such damages).

The techniques and approaches described in this book may not be suitable for everyone, and the reader should use their own judgment in determining their appropriateness. The author and publisher shall not be liable for any loss or damage caused or alleged to be caused directly or indirectly by the use or reliance on any of the techniques or approaches described in this book.

This book is intended to provide general information on the subject matter covered. It is not intended to provide specific legal, financial, or other professional advice, and should not be relied upon as such. If expert assistance is required, the services of a competent professional should be sought.

Increase Your Chances

The activities in this book are mainly composed of carefully designed questions and specific techniques with sequential instructions. The questions guide you through a structured and intentional reflection on your thoughts, behaviors, and beliefs. Examining these patterns of thought and behavior can provide insights into the underlying beliefs and ideas that are shaping your experiences: thoughts, feelings, and reactions. The sequence in which you respond to these questions is extremely important. We recommend that you do not skim the content or try to jump ahead before answering earlier questions. Responding to these questions wholeheartedly, even if it is difficult and taxing some of the time, can help your unconscious mind purge old limiting beliefs and form healthier patterns of thinking and behavior. That is the goal of therapy, and by seeking only knowledge without fully engaging with these ideas, you are passing up significant opportunities to evolve and become the person you know you are capable of becoming.

All of these exercises and questions are designed to help you establish a routine of thinking and communicating in an open, nonjudgmental manner. When you're able to look inward without criticism, you develop a more nuanced and thorough comprehension of your unrevealed core beliefs, behavioral patterns, and understandings. Honesty without judgment can assist you in identifying the root causes of these beliefs and comprehending how they affect your current reality. Later in the book, you'll see how this insight can be used to construct strategies for overcoming the limiting beliefs and forming healthier patterns of thinking and behavior, which in turn alter how you feel and how you interact with others. In other words, you move out of a destructive and dysfunctional cycle of self-defeat and into a new cycle that is productive and helpful in bringing about the experiences you desire most. That new cycle is where you give yourself permission to accept yourself more fully and cultivate more compassion for yourself, making it easier to deal with the inevitable difficulties we all face in life at some point or another. There is absolutely no risk on your end. To put it plainly, we won't be asking you to participate in any sort of social activity. You won't be given any assignments that require you to interact with strangers in public. This book contains a wide range of mental and physical exercises; however, you may want to do them in private, with no one around.

If you have any questions or comments, or you're in need for a personal advice - we'd love to hear from you. Contact us at www.ericks.org

Fear of Rejection: NLP Tools You Can Use

1st edition

ISBN: 978-80-87518-14-4

Manufactured in the United States of America.

Fear of Rejection

NLP Tools You Can Use

Shlomo Vaknin

Erickson Institute

What Brought You Here, Exactly?

In the space provided below, describe your reasoning for selecting this book as freely as possible. What were you thinking when you decided to address this issue at this point in your life? What was your most distressing realization about your rejection anxiety? What outcome from using the techniques in this book would be most important to you, aside from "getting over my fear of rejection"?

Contents

Related Books You May Want To Read

The BIG Book of NLP, Expanded: 350+ Techniques, Patterns & Strategies of Neuro Linguistic Programming

Erickson Institute | ISBN - 8087518055 | 550 pages

The new 12th edition for 2022, a must have for any student or practitioner. Now in a bigger page format and completely rewritten and edited for clarity and easier application. Dozens of new techniques added, as well as summary outlines for complex patterns.

NLP: The 57 Meta-Programs

Erickson Institute | ISBN - 8087518071 | 256 pages

The Meta-Programs model is essential for understanding and applying the effective communication patterns of NLP. Learn how to recognize your own and other people's habitual thinking patterns. In a concise and clear language, this book shows you practical ways to use the meta-programs for persuasion and rapport.

Advanced NLP Techniques for Therapists & Coaches

Erickson Institute | ISBN 808751811X | 200 pages

This is an advanced, modern NLP manual for therapists and coaches who want to expand and update their skills. You'll find advise about resistance, preparation for change work, and we cover a few dozens of new and powerful methods such as Vision-Down Stream, Targeting, Body Scan, Echo Events.

The Big Book of Self-Analysis: Discover Your Untapped Potential

Erickson Institute | ISBN - 9788087518120 | 500 pages

Self-discovery can be a healing process in and of itself. A workbook that can help you uncover the unconscious mental activities that shape your thoughts and behavior. Find out what your core beliefs are, both positive and negative. Set a timeline for your life and prepare for the future.

NLP: Start Here

Erickson Institute | ISBN - 8087518039 | 220 pages

An in-depth introduction to NLP, which includes chapters on the CNS, internal maps, modalities and sub-modalities, learning styles, and other basic concepts.

Signs You're Suffering From Rejection Anxiety

• Avoidance of social situations or events where rejection may be a possibility

• Feeling constantly inferior to others - a shortage of equality interpersonally

• Difficulty making and maintaining close relationships

• Difficulty expressing one's thoughts, feelings, or needs to others

• Difficulty setting boundaries or asserting oneself

• Difficulty accepting compliments or positive feedback

• Constant worry about not being good enough and thus risking getting rejected

• Difficulty making decisions or taking risks

• Low self-esteem or feelings of inadequacy

• Difficulty trusting others or forming close attachments

• Difficulty being vulnerable or open with others

• Difficulty being genuine in social situations, a preference to imitate others over being authentic

• Difficulty forming or maintaining romantic relationships

• Difficulty speaking up or expressing opinions in group settings

• Difficulty initiating or maintaining professional or personal projects or goals

• Physical symptoms such as increased heart rate, sweating, or difficulty breathing in social situations

• Difficulty sleeping or experiencing nightmares related to rejection

• Difficulty focusing or concentrating due to worry about rejection

• Difficulty making new friends or initiating social interactions

• Difficulty feeling confident or self-assured in social situations

• Difficulty feeling comfortable or accepted in one's own skin or with one's own identity

- Difficulty expressing affection or vulnerability in relationships

- Difficulty being assertive or standing up for oneself

- Difficulty relaxing or feeling at ease in social situations

- Feelings of shame or self-blame when rejected

- Difficulty being open to new experiences or challenges due to fear of rejection

- Other symptoms you experience:

Rejection Stinks

There is no doubt that rejection as a real-life, albeit fleeting, experience stings (and stinks). Fear of rejection is even worse because it is self-initiated as a reaction to fictitious scenarios, and it is frequently a detriment to your efforts to improve your life and achieve your most desired outcomes. It forcibly prevents you from living fully in the present moment, from taking risks that are worth the occasional failure, from approaching people you find attractive or interesting, from asserting yourself, from demanding what you deserve, from feeling whole as you are right now, and from doing so much more. Fear of rejection has evolved from a quick survival tactic in your youth to a crippling crutch and, eventually, an impenetrable concrete wall in your psyche with no doors or windows.

When you're anxious about being rejected, you could try to hide it or make up for it in other ways. You may resort to passive-aggressiveness, inactivity, or people-pleasing out of fear of being rejected. Moreover, it might make it hard to be yourself in social situations by undermining your authenticity.

In addition to hindering your professional and personal development, a fear of rejection can damage your friendships and intimate relationships. Fear of rejection can have a significant impact on your ability to thrive in a variety of personal and professional contexts; however, its impact varies from person to person.

Everyone, regardless of who they are, at some point in their lives, experiences rejection. Someone whose opinion of you matters to you, even if only a little bit, is saying something degrading about you, and you care about what they think of you. Someone criticizes your shoes, your gestures, your accent, your crooked tooth, your lack of focus, your lack of knowledge of world history, your dreams, your values, and your beliefs, and so on and so forth. You may be socially titled with humiliating nicknames, or your birth name may be twisted and deformed in order to further isolate you from ever feeling accepted and appreciated among your peers, coworkers, or even your own family of origin. Both of these tactics are intended to prevent you from ever feeling accepted and appreciated. They keep you lower on the social status ladder than they are and make you feel like an unwanted outsider by using words to cast a spell of rejection on you.

It is possible for you to give words an unfavorable connotation in your mind. However, words (as a digital format of perception) are just one of the many components that make up your experience of reality. Depending on how it is delivered and the situation in which it is used (context), the same word can mean either a cruel mockery or a playful and affectionate teasing. If you are in a vulnerable body-mind state at the time, your mind will interpret comments like "you're the worst" and "you're such a ***t!" very differently if someone angrily shouts them at you, than when they are made in jest by friends on a night out.

Beyond words and vocal pitches, you may feel rejected and insulted if someone looks at you sideways, dismisses your heartfelt plea with a dismissing wave of their hand, or displays the length of their middle finger. These are all non-verbal cues that communicate rejection and insult. Even though it is impolite to do so, turning around and making an unflattering face at you communicates very clearly and without words that you are not welcome in their line of sight and that they would rather ignore you entirely.

The act of being physically rejected, such as by being shoved and pushed around, can be harmful if allowed to be manifested as an emotional experience as well. Being told you can't take that seat on the school bus, being bullied, assaulted, or laughed at, stumbling and collapsing after someone deliberately places an obstacle in front of your feet, and other similar situations are all examples of social rejection.

One thing is shared by each of the aforementioned potentials for multi-sensory rejection: When these behaviors are carried out on purpose, they are intended to achieve one goal: to cause you to lose your balance, physically, mentally, and emotionally, in order to keep you under control and miserable, and they are most successful when they instill fear of rejection within the core of your being. Then you will never be a master, and you will never pose a threat to anyone's social status. You will always be a slave, the harmless weakling nobody pays real attention to.

You know this to be true: It's time to let go of your fear of rejection because you're hurting more and more if you continue to let any of the following symptoms ruin your experience of the one life you have. Mark the ones that feel true:

☐ Regardless of how hard you try, you feel less valuable and appreciated than certain other people.

☐ You are afraid of being criticized and invalidated, so you find it difficult to express yourself.

☐ You're a people-pleaser who derives self-esteem from the approval of others.

☐ As an adult, you feel threatened and intimidated by society's expectations of you.

☐ Even if you don't agree with people around you, you act in a way to blend in.

☐ You are plagued by self-doubt and judgmental thoughts on a regular basis.

☐ You take everything personally, even if it is obvious that the criticism has nothing to do with you.

☐ When you reflect on the rejection you've faced throughout your life, it appears that one experience led to another, and they all have one thing in common: you, and thus you are to blame.

☐ You react inappropriately to any hint that you might be rejected.

☐ When you are socially excluded, the feeling of being left out causes you to feel inherently different (or weird, or strange, or isolated).

☐ You find it difficult to be open and honest with people because you are afraid of being ridiculed.

☐ You genuinely think you have a low sense of self-esteem.

☐ You frequently misinterpret mild, constructive criticism for a rude and violent attack on your character.

☐ You frequently feel as if you are making decisions, plans, or choices in response to previous traumas rather than investing in how you truly want to live.

☐ You are plagued with self-doubt and a weak sense of your own true identity. In other words, you don't know yourself very well and don't trust your own instincts.

☐ Certain words, looks, or actions appear to elicit a reactionary defensive response in you that appears to be beyond your conscious control.

☐ You try too hard to blend in rather than stand out because you lack a strong sense of self-worth.

☐ As a child, you were hypersensitive and easily overwhelmed, and that oversensitivity and excessive stimulation have become ingrained in your adult mind and psyche.

☐ Most of the time, you realize that you misinterpreted someone else's words or actions and mistook them for an insult.

☐ You are constantly concerned with what others think of you and are extremely self-conscious.

☐ You suffer mentally and emotionally from a lack of perceived interpersonal equality.

☐ You would rather imitate others than be yourself.

☐ You are socially awkward and spend a lot of time alone.

☐ You frequently recall memories from your early childhood or adolescence of being rejected, ridiculed, abused, violated, or betrayed by significant people in your life, such as parents, caregivers, close friends, teachers, and so on.

☐ When someone rejects you, you experience physiological and psychological dissonance.

☐ In the end, all you ever wanted was the one thing that eluded you: to be accepted, loved, respected, and cared about.

Fear of Rejection Is a Learned Reaction

As humans we're capable of one-trial learning, directly and indirectly. A baby only needs to touch the hot stove once in order to never ever touch it again. That's a direct, self initiated and self taught learning experience.

My uncle was a high-security prison warden, and as young children he took myself and my cousins to tour the facilities he was in charge of. He showed us first hand how the hardcore prisoners were living, and he especially made a point to show us the drug-addict prisoners in solitude that were in the midst of their worst withdrawal. The whole field-trip must have taken less than an hour, and yet even in our last year's family reunion we all agreed it is still ongoing in our minds. Even though we all grew up in a relatively poor and under-developed drug-infested city, to working class parents and had to work extremely hard to get out of there - nobody in my extended family has ever resorted to either crime nor drugs, not even recreational drugs.

The horrid sights, smells and sounds from that single visit are still fresh in our minds, many decades later. That's an indirect, and still highly influential learning experience. The bottom line is: humans can learn instantly. And we can learn the fastest how to avoid potential pain. That's what my uncle has given myself and my cousins as a lifelong present that keeps on giving. We avoided the pain of incarceration and loss of freedom, and the pain of addiction and violence, even when the temptations were high and the perceived risks were low.

Your fear of rejection is also a learned experience, and most likely a direct one. You were rejected at least once during your formative years, and that has left a mark on your psyche with a rapid fire pain prevention reaction: activate avoidance before it's too late. While this pain avoidance strategy is quite helpful for leading a respectable and responsible adult life, it is quite a hindrance when it comes to taking calculated risks that at worst may cause some emotional disturbance, such as a temporary embarrassment or just feeling down for a little while.

Rejection and the fear of rejection are both nominalizations. It's a word or a term that describes a wide range of emotional experiences, but it's not precise enough to explain and resolve the exact mind-body state you're in as you relive the memories of the original hurtful experience, and by doing so, you indirectly instill the fear of rejection with importance and power.

 As you might expect, this is a never-ending cycle, with each reaction feeding the next phase even more.

As an individual, what does it mean to you when you're rejected? How do you personally interpret rejection?

Fear of Rejection Causes You To Act in Ways That Make You Feel and Look Weak, Incompetent, and Disturbed

Humans have an innate desire to feel accepted and included, and as a result, they often act in ways that facilitate this urge. Although there are certain benefits to adopting the style, vocabulary, and norms of one's peers, excessive conformity can have negative consequences. You may feel pressured to act in ways that go against your values in order to maintain social acceptance.

Body language changes brought on by rejection anxiety are sometimes misread as signs of inferiority. People who suffer from this anxiety sometimes come across as weak and insecure, despite the fact that confidence and an image of authority are crucial in many situations. If you have a problem dealing with rejection, it could be preventing you from negotiating the best possible terms for your employment.

Because of our social nature, it is expected of us to behave politely and appropriately in public. If you have a problem with social rejection, you can find it difficult to strike up conversations with complete strangers or even "safe" acquaintances of friends. Your desire to isolate yourself could hamper your ability to form meaningful relationships with others.

Those who are particularly sensitive to rejection may find asking for or even being on first dates very nerve-wracking. It's easy to spend a whole date preoccupied with the question of whether or not your date likes you rather than concentrating on actually getting to know them and determining whether or not you'd like to go on another date with them. Problems communicating, worrying excessively about one's looks, an inability to eat, and an obviously anxious temperament are all symptoms of anxiety.

Having a spouse means engaging in a never-ending cycle of bargaining and giving in. It's unrealistic to expect a partner to share your views on every issue, no matter how well you get along. Those who are sensitive to criticism have a hard time advocating for themselves and asking for what they desire.

For many careers, the pressure to make a good impression does not subside once you've landed the job. Many occupations require social skills, the ability to negotiate and handle contracts, technical expertise, and the ability to pitch an idea to potential clients or investors. For those who are extremely sensitive to criticism, even the act of picking up the phone can be a terrible experience.

Rejection anxiety, ironically, frequently manifests as actual rejection. Confidence, according to mainstream psychology, is a key factor in attracting others. We are more likely to be rejected because we lack confidence due to our fear of rejection. As far as our competitive advantage goes, studies reveal that confidence is almost as crucial as intelligence.

Rejection anxiety causes you to act in ways that make you look weak, incompetent, and preoccupied. You may start to perspire excessively, tremor uncontrollably, fidget, avoid making eye contact, and find yourself unable to communicate clearly. These are just some of the possible reactions to such events; of course, everyone has their own unique pattern of responses.

Rejection-phobic people will go to great lengths to avoid conflict. It's possible that you're reluctant to express your wants and needs. To ignore or deny one's own needs is a typical coping mechanism. If you're too worried about what other people will think of you, you might never realize your true potential. Putting oneself out there is scary for everyone, but those who are especially sensitive to criticism may freeze up entirely. Even if you're unhappy with your existing circumstances, resisting change can feel safe.

Some people feed off of other people's insecurities. Those who are sensitive to criticism are more vulnerable to being used as pawns in a game of dominance. Expert manipulators often appear charming, sophisticated, and compassionate because they are well-versed in the social cues that elicit a favorable response. A master manipulator also knows how to keep someone who is extremely sensitive to rejection on edge, as if the manipulator were about to abandon them at any moment. Once the manipulator has gotten what they want out of the other person, they will almost always leave.

You feel a lack of authenticity. Rejection-phobic people tend to live their lives according to strict routines and predetermined scripts. It's common to hide who you really are for fear of being judged negatively. This can give off the impression that you're not being genuine, which can lead to a hardened resistance to life's adversities.

Some people who are afraid of being rejected have a hard time being themselves around others and resort to passive-aggressive behavior since they can't completely ignore their own wants and desires. You might put off starting work or finishing tasks, make excuses for not completing them, grumble about your workload, and generally be inefficient.

It is human nature to want to provide for those we care about, but people who are overly concerned about being rejected may go too far. It's likely that you'll have a hard time rejecting an offer, even if doing so will put you through significant personal suffering. People-pleasers often take on too much, putting themselves in danger of depression. Overdoing it in the interest of pleasing others might lead to complicity in abusive behavior.

Generally speaking, would you say that humans are good? What makes you say so?

People who are afraid of being rejected are less likely to manipulate others and more likely to offer a helping hand. Keep an eye out for indicators that the people closest to you want you to be more forceful, whether it's through encouraging you to open up to them or probing you about how you really feel. However, those who are sensitive to rejection often interpret such attempts as emotionally menacing. Because of this, those closest to you may tread carefully so as not to further exacerbate your anxiety. As time goes on, they may grow increasingly irritated and upset, eventually confronting you about your behavior or pulling away emotionally.

Your fear of rejection may evolve into a fear of abandonment, which may lead to resentment or mistrust in your relationships with your spouse, family and other important individuals in your life. This might manifest in harmful ways, such as constantly peeking at your partner's phone or social media to see what they've been up to. You may want to use a pencil to jot down your thoughts as you go through the following questions, as your answers may change later in the process. How does rejection anxiety affect you today? Just how much of an impact does fearing of being rejected have on your daily life?

Where do you draw the line between a healthy fear of rejection and an unrealistic one?

If someone rejects you, what does that say about you?

This next question is certainly not an easy one, but try your best to answer it intuitively. How exactly would you determine when the time has come to stop worrying about being rejected and move on to other responsibilities?

Even if It's Only in Your Mind, It's Still Ruining Your Life

You may have tried less effective approaches to dealing with rejection anxiety, such as attempting to "accept yourself," meditation, ruminating on past hurt, rationalizing the reasons you may fear other people's reactions to you, forcing yourself to do things that trigger the anxiety, or self-helping in other ways.

All of these popular but ineffective approaches have failed for a reason. It's because you were attempting to solve a deeply rooted issue on the surface.It's like swimming and then finding yourself drifting at sea, fighting against a strong current. When you can't swim back to shore, that is the worst approach to take, as any lifeguard will tell you. You will eventually exhaust yourself and drown.

Why does this approach consistently fail? Because fear of rejection is nothing more than a learned knee-jerk reaction to specific or generalized external stimuli, which is then internally interpreted to imply meaning higher up (meta) than its original perception by your five human senses. All of these perplexing terms will be explained shortly.

The therapeutic approach, which we wholeheartedly support and has proven to be effective and successful, is to train your mind to efficiently screen sensory input from the environment and process it appropriately in the service of your desired outcomes and future selves. For decades, NLP and Ericksonian therapy have advocated for just that, with great success.

The field of Neuro Linguistic Programming (NLP) arose from the modeling of the actions and thought processes of extraordinary people from various disciplines, most notably the most prominent and successful therapists (Dr. Milton H. Erickson, Fritz Perls and Virginia Satir). NLP has established approaches and criteria for identifying and describing unique, repeatable patterns in ultra-effective role models' language and actions. NLP modeling approaches entail detecting a person's mental strategies ("Neuro") by examining that person's language structures ("Linguistic") and nonverbal expressions. The results of this study then were incorporated into step-by-step strategies or protocols ("Programming") that are being used to teach the expertise to others and use it effectively in varying situations.

NLP teaches us to recognize and value our unique qualities and ways of thinking, but it also suggests that we can gain insight from the experiences of others because our neurological systems are so alike. We can gain much from the programs developed by others as well. NLP places a premium on practical application, which is arguably its most crucial feature. The principles and methods of NLP are meant to be easily perceptible; therefore, training programs and NLP principles prioritize interactive, experiential learning environments. Also, because NLP procedures are based on successful human models, their worth and underlying structures are frequently immediately apparent to even those with no training.

As the field of NLP grew further, that investigation into the workflows of these remarkable therapists has revealed sequences and strategies (protocols) that can be used to teach patients how to work out their own issues. The ones that proved to be the most effective in our 20 plus years of experience as private therapists are what we share with you in this book. We'll keep the jargon to a minimum, and yet we still need to discuss the most essential elements of NLP, so that you can use it appropriately.

There may be many areas of overlap between the skills of effective therapists and those of effective teachers, leaders, and managers, despite the fact that at first impression, a model based on the interaction skills of competent therapists may not seem applicable to other areas such as business, education, or leadership. Although there may be just a slight resemblance, the modeling techniques utilized to extract the significant therapeutic behaviors of these outstanding therapists can also be used to uncover the psychological, behavioral, and linguistic patterns of remarkable executives, educators, and leaders. Training, communication, persuasion, sales, public speaking, negotiation, creativity, innovation, entrepreneurship, organizational development, corporate consulting, leadership, and many other facets of education and management have all benefited from NLP's research into the impact of cognitive and emotional strategies, language patterns, and mindsets.

NLP is based on a set of basic assumptions about people and reality that have significant impacts on everything we do as humans. To evaluate and uncover significant patterns of beliefs, behavior, and interconnectedness, NLP provides a set of principles and distinctions that are ideally suited for practical and verifiable applications. It is predicated on a number of rather simple, explicit linguistic, neurobiological, and behavioral patterns and distinctions that are more fundamental and content-free than any other extant model of human cognition and behavior. With the help of NLP, we can go beyond the obvious actions people take and into the deeper motivations and mental models that drive their actions. By its very name, Neuro Linguistic Programming suggests the convergence of three distinct scientific disciplines.

From the moment you wake up and right until you fall asleep at night, the world is bombarding you with an endless stream of sensory stimuli. You see, hear, touch, being touched by, smell and taste the environment outside your organism - your whole body. Your own eyes are the physical extension of your brain.

In NLP, the "neuro" refers to the central nervous system. Understanding and using the concepts and patterns of the neurological system is central to your recovery. As NLP explains, thinking, memorizing, generating, and the ability to visualize are all products of protocols run by the human nervous system. Everything we know comes from the mixing and matching of the data our brains take in and analyze. This is related to how we use the five senses (sight, touch, sound, as well as smell and taste) as translated internally, after processing the incoming stimuli passively via the five physical senses through which we experience the world.

NLP also makes use of insights from linguistics. The NLP perspective holds that while language may have its origins in the neurological system, it also actively influences and directs neural processing. Certainly, one's ability to use language to activate or excite the neurological systems of others is one of the most significant tools at one's disposal. Therefore, the ability to explain, induce, and articulate ideas, objectives, and concerns pertinent to an activity or context is fundamental to clear communication and cooperation. What's left is the idea of programming.

NLP is predicated on the hypothesis that all mental processes, including those involved in learning, remembering, and being creative, can be reduced to a set of programs—specifically, sets of neurolinguistic programs that are more or less efficient at achieving their intended aims and objectives. The assumption is that human beings have preprogrammed responses to the world around them. Our reactions to challenges and our perspectives on new ideas are shaped by the mental programs we've trained ourselves to rely on, and not all programs are equally represented. When it comes to completing certain functions, some methods or applications tend to do better than most others. Since NLP integrates elements from the neurological, linguistic, and cognitive sciences, it shares some ground with other approaches to psychology. It is also based on system theory and programming concepts. Its goal is to unify many scientific models and hypotheses. NLP's strength lies in the fact that it unifies various theoretical frameworks.

The term "modeling" is used to describe the process by which most NLP methods and resources have been derived. NLP has primarily modeled efficient behavior and the mental processes that underpin it.Analyzing language patterns ("linguistic") and non-verbal communication, NLP modeling seeks to learn about the functioning of the brain ("neuro"). Following this evaluation, process procedures or programs ("programming") are developed that can be used to teach the skill to others or adapt it for usage in different contexts.

When it comes to NLP, the map is not the territory. Since we humans have to gather information about the world through limited sensory input, we can never hope to have a comprehensive understanding of the world. The bird's sensory system is fundamentally different from ours, so when it looks at this page, it will have a totally different experience than we will.

The information we acquire through our senses and the connections we make between that information and our personal memories and other experiences are the only tools we have for creating maps of the world around us. This means that rather than reacting to the world as it is, we react to the world as we have constructed it in our brains. From this point of view, there is no one map of the world that is "absolutely correct" or "accurate." Each of us has a unique perspective on the world, which is shaped by the specific neurolinguistic maps we've developed over the years. Our interpretations and reactions to the world around us, as well as the significance we assign to our actions and experiences, will be determined more by our neurolinguistic maps than by the external environment. Therefore, it is not the outward world that confines, frees, or otherwise affects us, but rather the mental map we have constructed of it.

To illustrate, no one would dispute your subjective experience if you went around with a knife stuck in your chest and said you were experiencing pain there. If they can make reference to what you're going through, they'll be able to validate your pain, express sympathy, and so on. They don't have to take your word for it that you're hurting; they can see with their own eyes that you are. Put simply, a knife to the chest is not a nominalization. On the other hand, your mental world (where your subjective experiences operate) is invisible and inaccessible to anyone else's. In the external world, outside your organism, your fears do not exist; they do not occupy space, not even a microscopic one. They still have a significant effect on your subjective experience (by influencing your behavior). However, your fear of being rejected may or may not become active, and thus may or may not be a part of your subjective experience. You can't just will the physical knife out of existence.

With some strategic thinking (NLP tools) and an honest effort, your fear of rejection can become less powerful and have less of an impact on your experience of life. Due to its nominal nature, fear can be conceptualized in a variety of ways, unlike the knife. The only thing you have to do to overcome your fear is to learn to use your mind wisely.

One of the key tenets of NLP is that, by expanding one's mental "map," one can better understand the range of options available to them within their current reality. NLP resources and methods are most useful when applied to expanding our mental maps of the world. An essential tenet of NLP is that the more complete your cognitive map is, the more choices you'll have for responding to any difficulties you encounter in actual reality.

False assumptions about other people's motivations are something everyone has experienced. Think back on at least three times in the recent past when you misunderstood someone's words or actions and allowed yourself to become offended or rejected before realizing your error in judgment.

What was the difference between your mental map and the territory (current reality)?

NLP additionally assumes, with good reason, that both the mind and the body are systemic processes. In other words, we are a system within a succession of larger systems, and each of these systems is a system composed of many sub-systems. Interactions within an individual and between individuals and their surroundings are systemic and follow certain systemic rules. So many systems and subsystems that make up our organisms, our relations, and our civilizations are interconnected and have an effect on one another. The parts of a system are all interconnected, so it's impossible to separate them totally. Numerous factors in a given system can have an impact on an individual's behavior. One must consider not only the internal processes occurring but also the external systems' effects on the person being observed. For instance, an individual or procedure that functions well in one system or setting may encounter constraints or problems while transitioning to another. All the connections between factors that are prompting, stimulating, and affecting a certain occurrence or process must be taken into account.

In order to read, recognize elements, and apply interventions to your mental maps, we use in NLP a special mind-body state called "downtime." The term "downtime" refers to a state of relaxation and mental clarity that allows you to process information and experiences more effectively. During downtime, the mind is less cluttered and more open to new ideas and insights. There is nothing mysterious about downtime; it is how we define the blissful state of "flow." It occurs when the conscious mind is less occupied with random associations and more attuned to the task at hand. Close your eyes and take a few deep breaths. As you exhale, let go of any tension or strain you may have felt in your body. Focus your attention on learning to deal with your fear of rejection. Imagine yourself talking to your inner wisdom or a wise and understanding guide or mentor. Ask this inner wisdom to help you understand the lessons that you can learn from this book. When you are ready, slowly open your eyes and return to your present surroundings. What you've done in less than a minute is access a downtime state. You can access such a state in a variety of ways, and throughout this book we'll show you how.

There is a law in systems theory known as the "Law of Requisite Variety." This is a fundamental idea that underpins all excellent performance. The Law of Requisite Variety implies that we must consistently explore variations in the processes and operations we use to achieve outcomes. A change in context or supporting system can render even the most successful methods obsolete. Achievement may be both a springboard for further innovation and a trap that stifles new ideas. Assuming something will continue to be effective only because it has been successful in the past is a common fallacy. What used to work, however, may no longer do so if the underlying system undergoes a transformation. According to the Law of Requisite Variety, "in order to successfully adapt and live, a member of a system needs a certain minimum amount of flexibility, and that flexibility has to be proportional to the potential variation or the uncertainty in the rest of the system." Which is to say, if one is truly dedicated to achieving a particular outcome, then that person should have access to a variety of routes leading to that desired outcome. The level of flexibility available within the system in which the intention is to be achieved determines the number of possibilities that must be considered to be confident that the desired outcome can be realized.

The key is to evaluate the interdependencies between the various components of a system to arrive at an accurate estimate of the degree of flexibility needed. Flexibility is especially important in dynamic circumstances and contexts. One more thing we can infer from the Law of Requisite Variety is that the component of a system with the greatest degree of flexibility is also the component with the greatest potential to accelerate change within the system. How to strike a balance between flexibility and other qualities, such as consistency and congruence in action, is a major problem in performance improvement.

The answer is in the placement of the flexibility. One must be adaptable in the means by which they achieve their goals if they are to be consistent with regard to those goals. The question is how flexible we are in our execution. To some extent, your level of flexibility depends on the areas in which you've already decided you can't be flexible.

Consider your experience of current reality. It is what you consciously perceive at this vey moment, and at any moment you interact directly with your environment - what happens right here and now, externally (outside your body) and internally (inside your body and mind). On purpose we do not call it "the present moment" because, if you'd think about it, you do not live entirely in the present moment as if you're an enlightened one of the legendary oracles. You're lost in thoughts more often than being fully engaged with your body and kinesthetic senses.

You use your mind to think and analyze and ponder and recall and plan and construct digital verbal language (words, self talk) and non-verbal language (mental images and movies) and you are able to create infinite new and amazing worlds, concepts and other mental constituents literally by sleight of intentional thought. You live most of the time inside your head and not out there in current reality. There is a good reason for that.

You are in contact with (and make sense of) the world through your senses. The visual sensory system has a significant evolutionary advantage and is possibly the most complex and developed sense in humans. The auditory system is the primary sensory modality for enabling human communication. The vestibular sense informs your brain about your body's orientation in space in relation to gravity. During physical activity, the kinesthetic sense collects continuous sensory feedback about what is going on within, through, and on your body. Perception is the process of taking in and making sense of information that comes from the senses.

Day and night, the world bombards us with an infinite number of stimuli that our underpowered brains are unable to process. Much like a computer's processor, our brain must process the data coming in from the senses in order to keep up with the demands of regular living. According to Broadbent's Filter Theory of Attention, this type of filtering occurs much before the meaning of the input is analyzed. Even input that you do not pay direct attention to is processed in some way (unconsciously). To a certain extent, our vision is limited to what is immediately in front of us. The frequency range of the human ear is 20 to 20,000 Hz. The mosquito's bite isn't felt by our kinesthetic senses until it's too late. Our receptors are limited, and so we do not experience the entire scope of available bits of information (events). That is the first filter that is acted upon our central nervous system.

Consciousness has its bounds. In particular, in our current awareness of reality, humans are limited to a finite number of bits of information. George A. Miller meticulously presents the boundaries of consciousness in the "Magic Number" 7, plus or minus 2. His research shows that we can hold seven pieces of data in our heads at once, plus or minus two. Miller's paper contains an intriguing implication: chunk size is variable. That is, 7 (+ or -) 2 is a restriction on the number of chunks (which can be groupings of bits) rather than the number of bits (single sensory inputs). As a result, by carefully designing the code that organizes our conscious experience, we can greatly expand the amount of data we can consciously represent to ourselves. His description of a chunk is purposefully vague.

In general, unless it is very distinct, urgent, or personally relevant, new information or an external stimulus that is not consciously in focus will go unnoticed. Visual attention serves an evolutionary purpose by speeding up the process of locating specific objects in a cluttered visual environment. Consider our ancestors, who had to keep an eye out for dangers such as the tiger lurking in the bushes. In most cases, we don't even realize that this level of sophisticated processing is taking place within us. The process of pre-atentive processing occurs in the brain after certain sensory inputs have arrived from the senses (eyes, ears, and skin) but before we become consciously aware of them.

Through a process called perceptual organization, we are able to give meaning to the world around us. Our brains work hard to make sense of all the information coming in from our senses and deliver only the most crucial details to our awareness. The state of being fully aware of something involves paying close and undivided attention to that something. Awareness of one's own internal and external perceptions constitutes the foundational level of consciousness.

At the second level of consciousness, we take a step back from the physical world and the constraints of time and space to reflect on what we know and do with symbolic knowledge like language and mental representation. Self-awareness, the recognition that one is conscious and capable of introspection, is the highest level of consciousness. Organic bodily functions like digestion, respiration, hormone secretion, liver synthesis, and so on take place automatically and unconsciously.

We can only process about 5-7 pieces of data in our conscious mind at once. When you're deep in thought about what to eat for lunch, you may not even notice the tightness in your lower back or the background hum of the AC. Although you do not presently perceive them, these sensory inputs are still reaching your receptors. The part of your mind that deals with things you aren't consciously aware of but which are still part of your actual experience is called your unconscious.

Simply put, the unconscious is everything you are not aware of right now. As soon as you recognize it, it gains awareness. This is true for actual events that occur around you, such as the air conditioner or the curtains moving in the autumn breeze. This holds true not just for external events but also for internal processes like digestion, the emergence of limiting beliefs, and the awakening of a fear of rejection.

You can't change something you don't know exists. You can't heal from hurt feelings or overcome self-limiting beliefs if you don't know how exactly they work within your psyche. When we learn to recognize and respond methodically to patterns in our experience, we can render unconscious certain aspects of our experience that we previously had to manage at the level of consciousness. Consciousness chunks consist of patterns and repetitions that have not yet been rendered unconscious. Because of this, the initial chunk size when learning a new task will be very small and only contain a transitory pattern or predictability from our prior experience.

When raw input data (sights, sounds, sensations, tastes, and smells) enters your sensory receptors, it is processed through a series of filters to separate what is important from what is not. The representational system (in NLP) refers to the format in which data is accepted by your central nervous system. A representational system is how we internally perceive what we outwardly sense. It could be something we hear, taste, feel, see, smell, or even taste. Whatever it is, we refer to it as "information." We call it "information" because it can be processed and utilized by the mind. Usually the smell is the first indicator that breakfast is burning. Information is conveyed by smell. Another term for the representational system is sense modality.

The significance of representational systems lies in the fact that they serve as the basis for the codification of our experiences. They are the primary building blocks of our thoughts and behaviors. You can trace it all back to them. Utilizing representational systems, we encode or assimilate our experiences and perspectives. This data is then accessed again when needed, using the very same representational systems. This process is known as "retrieving" or "accessing" the data.

Representational systems have the advantage of being much more comprehensive than just how information enters your brain. With just your brainpower, you can relive and reflect on past experiences as well as generate brand-new ones. Accordingly, you have a visual representational system (images), an auditory representational system (sounds), a kinesthetic representational system (body sensations), and an olfactory representational system (tastes and smells).

At least one of the sensory modalities must be used to process or access any given piece of information. If data is processed visually, it must be stored and recalled as mental pictures or movies. When information is taken in through the ear, it should be stored and retrieved in the form of audible or acoustic information. If we don't pay attention to a sound, it may end up sounding more like white noise in our memory, and our imagination will fill in the gaps. The encoding or recall of feelings as sensations is essential if they are to be processed kinesthetically. Therefore, representational systems are synonymous with the senses because it is ideal for input and output to have the same format. While these general rules apply to all five senses, we focus on sight, hearing, and touch because those are the most widely used.

How we consciously employ our minds to make sense of the information we take in is another crucial aspect of representational systems. What we're using is our internal dialogue or the filtering of external feedback. This is known as the auditory digital representational

31

system. Digital being the symbols (agreed upon language, gestures, signs, etc.) we use for communication.

If you are not fluent in Japanese and find yourself in Tokyo, and an elderly Japanese man begins shouting at you, because you have no reference to what he says, the word he keeps repeating could have a wide range of meanings. You'll be perplexed, and you'll probably start looking around to figure out what he means. It's possible that the word and gesture are the highest form of respect he can offer you and are appropriate in his culture as a traditional Japanese honor. Alternatively, he may be insulting you with a nasty curse or trying to warn you that a bee is hovering behind your left ear. You won't be able to give that word any meaning in a digital representation system until you learn what it means.

The same gesture and word in English, however, would be translated very differently by your mind, wouldn't it? If he yelled at you, "Bee! Bee!" in English, you'd instinctively jump without thinking and look around your body to find the bee and avoid getting stung. In the second scenario, your brain processes the incoming data (a Japanese man shouting at you) much more quickly and almost instantly because your central nervous system has learned earlier what that English word plus that gesture may refer to and is activating autonomic behavioral responses to deal with potential danger (a bee), even though you are not yet consciously aware of it being present (as otherwise, the old Japanese man would not see the need to shout at you).

Now that you have a better understanding of how your brain processes information and makes adjustments to keep you safe in any type of scenario, you may be able to answer a challenging question: Did you used to (or do you still) believe that you are the center of your world and that everything that happens to you or through you is intentional and either meant to help you or harm you? To put it another way, is it possible that you often personalize input data even if it may not accurately reflect who you are? In response to this question, what thoughts and experiences came to mind?

A nominalization happens when the cognitive object exists in your mind (as a notion, a mental entity), but not in any external reality (environment) outside your mind. Your liver is an object in reality, although you cannot see it and even if you dd probably should not touch it. An apple is an object in reality, obviously. A satellite in space is an object in reality because you can (theoretically) touch it under certain circumstances. In traditional NLP training programs, we'd say that a word or term is a nominalization if we cannot theoretically place it inside a barrel (no matter how big that barrel has to be). "Love" is a nominalization; "electrical current" is not. While you cannot transfer your exact subjective notion of love to another person, no matter what you use, you can certainly electrocute them with the right tools.

Rejection as an internal experience is also a nominalization, as are all fears, desires, emotions, and thoughts. They exist only within the realm of your mental sphere, but never as an independent entity outside your mind. You cannot place rejection, or fear of rejection, inside a barrel, can you?

Just because we cannot take a fear and shove it into a wooden barrel does not mean that subjective experience is meaningless or less important than an object in physical reality. All we are saying is that there are additional steps between the perception of current reality and the physiological manifestation (body sensation) of the feeling we translate as "fear of rejection." And that's where you can exert some level of control over your subjective experience. It's not the "what" (content) that makes you nervous; it's the "how" (syntax and form) that makes you nervous. If you change how your mind processes stimuli and activates that fear of rejection in a specific context, you change the outcome - your experience in current reality.

We have established that our internal experience of reality, as it is right now (current reality), and of life, as it was (past) and as we wish it to be (future) or not (anxiety), is constructed with the building blocks of representational systems. There are organized sequences of sights, sounds, and sensations that create meaning inside your mind. Language serves as a mediator in translating raw sensory-based external and internal experiences to your present consciousnesses.

Modality is another term we use for a representational system. The sub-modalities are the qualities or attributes of a representational system. These are the characteristics of the primary modality. They are part of the representation, not separate entities. A sub-modality is the modality's "how." Size, or how large the internal image is, distance, or how far ahead the internal image is, brightness level, and other factors are examples of visual sub-modalities. Tone, pitch, distance, and direction are examples of auditory sub-modalities. Pressure, temperature, sensations, and so on are examples of kinesthetic sub-modalities.

The story line is the content communicated by the projected images and sounds when you watch a movie on TV. When you perceive these data inputs, you use both the visual and auditory modalities. The sub-modalities are the factors the director selected to use to present the data, such as whether the film is in black and white or color, how scenes are angled with the camera, point of view, sound effects and their direction, the tone of the dialogue and the pacing of the actors' actions, and the use of backdrops.

Though largely unconsciously and without conscious direction, you carry out the same operation in your mind. These automatic mental movies dictate how you feel (your state of mind) in the moment, just as the director manipulates the sub-modalities of his film to elicit specific emotional responses from the audience.

Sub-modalities can be thought of as the fundamental components of every sensory modality / representational system. Imagine looking at a cactus, for instance. You can close your eyes if it makes it easier to imagine. How sharp is the mental image, exactly? What is the light level or darkness level? Exactly how colorful was it? Or was it in black and white?

We were using the visual representational system because we asked you to imagine looking at a cactus. Clarity, brightness, and color saturation were the sub-modalities.

Let's give it a shot with the auditory representational system. Think about the sound of the birds singing in the garden. At what volume level did you hear the birds? How clear was the sound? Were they high-pitched? Was the sound soothing or sharp? It is possible to apply the same sub-modal analysis to multiple representational systems. Someone's use of the term "loud colors" does not refer to the audibility of the shades of green but rather to their predominance and intensity. In this context, "sharp" does not refer to a sound's ability to cause physical harm; rather, it describes the sound's edginess and, potentially, irritation. When someone says they're feeling blue, they're not referring to the color of their complexion. They are trying to convey that they are feeling down or sad.

Along with the kinesthetic representational system, there are kinesthetic sub-modalities. temperature, texture, and pressure, for example. Imagine having to take a cactus in both hands and move it across the room. You would want to do so carefully, of course, so you do not hurt yourself with its thorns.

How would it feel in your hands as you gently grabbed the plant? Is your body going to be relaxed or tense? How slowly would you move? What would be the texture of the cactus that you could feel in your hands as you lifted it in the air? Can you imagine how sharp the cactus' thorns would be?

Let's try now a synthesis of all representational systems. Let your mind wander to a scene where you are perched on top of a lovely hill and looking down at the green fields and trees below. Imagine a gust of wind passing right through you. Listen to the wind blow and observe the flowers as they sway in the breeze. Listen carefully, and you may be able to pick up on a cat's distant meowing and the dog's retaliatory barking. Take note of the vibrant colors of the grass, trees, and land. Imagine yourself gently touching the girth of an ancient oak tree. What does the texture feel like? Take a deep breath and inhale the scent of unspoiled trees, flowers, and grass. Here, have a leaf of basil from the plant next to you. What do you think of the flavor?

What causes you to be in a certain body-mind state is the sequential activation, in a specific context, of a set of representational systems, each with its own sub-modalities. In more philosophical terms, "I think; therefore, I am." What needs to be emphasized, though, is that "think" does not always refer to the digital processing of words and sentences. When we talk about "thinking," we mean all the mental operations (conscious and unconscious) performed by representational systems in response to sensory input.

Everything about you at any given time is part of your state. Being sad, happy, or excited are all good ways to describe someone's mental or emotional state. A person's "mind state" refers to their current mental status, including their mood, thoughts, level of concentration, and accessibility of mental resources. There is more to a state than just emotion. States have a tendency to make certain skill sets more accessible.

Have you ever realized that when you go through something unpleasant in life, you get to relive it over and over again in your mind? Let's say you and your friend had a fierce disagreement, and long after you left, you realized that you were still arguing a few hours later, but only within yourself. You lose track of time in pointless rumination because your friend is just no longer there at all. But that pointless ruminating has a consequence: a stress response, which means a chemical imbalance.

If you decide to think about a memory that made you feel strong emotions, you set in motion a chain reaction of representational systems that work together to retrieve the information from the unconscious part of your mind. You don't think about this memory all the time, nonstop. It is stored somewhere deep within your mind, and you must perform certain cognitive tasks in order to bring it back to your conscious mind and pay attention to its mental movie. In spite of the fact that the actual event occurred a long time ago, it continues to be acted out in your mind as though it were happening right now, with you in the middle of it all.

The three major representational systems are activated when you replay a memory as a mental movie: you see, hear, and feel the movie as if it were taking place in the present, even though it is taking place only in your head and not in the physical world. When these representational systems are activated in a systematic manner, a familiar body-mind state is manufactured by the playback.

While a typical psychologist would spend hours, if not years, dissecting the content of that memory and diagnosing the meaning of each element, the impact of that memory on you remains unchanged. It's still bothering you, and it's still affecting your day-to-day life, even though you know that the event in question happened a long time ago and is extremely unlikely to repeat itself at any point in the foreseeable future. One can therefore deduce that dwelling on one's past and trying to understand it are fruitless. It may make you feel better in the short term because you're acting as if you're taking action to fix your inner conflict, but ultimately, you realize sooner or later that you can't alter the events that have already occurred. It has happened as it has happened.

When compared to conventional methods, NLP and Ericksonian therapy take a very different approach. We focus on the here and now—on how your mind is currently retrieving and interpreting those emotionally charged memories. We don't try to change the memory's content but rather retrain the brain to retrieve it in a more effective manner. This method is being used for good reason, as it is the only one that is grounded in reality rather than fiction.

It's pointless to waste time trying to reason with yourself or convince yourself that there are good reasons for what's happened to you. On some level, you know that what you remember happened, and it happened exactly as you remember it. You were severely hurt, both emotionally and physically, as a result of the words and deeds of others. Let us now take your words about what happened verbatim and propose the following viewpoint.

Could it be that two people could share the same event, but one would be thrilled by it and the other would be terrified by it? Every one of us knows someone who seems to have been born with the ability to stand in front of a thousand people and deliver an interesting and informative lecture. Moreover, we know many people, perhaps including ourselves, who are petrified at the idea of performing in front of even a dozen people, let alone thousands. With a stage and a crowd, the setting is exactly the same. That is, it is not the content of the experience that determines whether you have a positive or negative reaction to it. It is how you process the idea of standing in front of a large crowd or recalling an emotionally charged past memory in the present moment.

Can you appreciate how two people can experience the same event in vastly different ways? Can you appreciate how two people can recall the same type of emotionally charged memory and one will experience overwhelming anxiety while the other will experience boredom and apathy?

Could you think of a time when someone responded to your story by sharing their own, and you were surprised to learn that they had experienced a similar challenge in the past but had emerged more resilient from it? They might have said something to the effect of "Yeah, the same thing happened to me; I was upset for a while, but later I just chose to shrug it off and move on with my life; why let anyone tell me who I am?"

Shrugging it off does not entail changing the content of a fixed past event, does it not? To "shrug it off," they accessed the emotionally charged memory in a new way and then made a behavioral choice to lessen the impact of the memory on their present reality. Do they have superhuman abilities? What special skills do they have that regular people don't? Naturally, that's not the case. Everyone has the ability to just shrug it off and move on. When you step outside and realize it's chillier than you anticipated, you shrug it off. What happens, happens, and you just have to deal with it. You might be upset for a few moments, but you'll be reasonable about it (and act maturely) and go about your business. The sudden chill won't ruin your day; it'll just mess with your mood for a little while until you make a choice about how to act in response to the discomfort.

Here is a difficult question: What makes a fictitious mental movie that only exists inside your mental sphere for a few moments any different than dealing with the cold weather outside?

The unexpected chill is not pleasant. It is unpleasant to recall an emotionally charged memory. In the here and now, the cold smacks you in the face. Similarly, your mind is flooded with the distressing memory, and it consumes your attention in the present moment. The cold is outside your body, but it quickly translates into kinesthetic discomfort. Once you recall the unpleasant experience, it quickly transforms from a visual and auditory movie into a kinesthetic bodily discomfort that was previously hidden deep in your unconscious mind. Each of these real-life experiences is generally undesirable, and you wouldn't miss any of them if they never happened again. One final fact: These events each last only for a brief period of time.

However, you let one overwhelm you while allowing the other to irritate you only slightly. You choose to have a slew of chemical imbalances with your memory because you believe it is the only way to deal with it, and you have little discomfort going out to meet the cold weather.

This lengthy discussion should lead you to the following conclusions: The first, most important tenet of subjectivity is that your internal experiences cannot be shared with anyone else because each person's nervous system interprets input stimuli differently (depending on context, of course). Second, because your life experience is subjective, the content of past events is less important than how they are recalled and processed in current reality. And third, you can respond in various ways to internal and external events by changing the sequence and form of the representational systems used to process the data, but only if you know how to do so effectively. It is certainly understandable that painful memories and the words of others bothered you up until this point. You just did not know better. Now you're putting the power over your own subjective experience back where it belongs: in your behavioral choices.

Our basic presupposition, that all behavior is the result of learned (habitual) responses (which are consequences of behavioral choices combined with one-trial learning), has a number of ramifications, as we will explore throughout this book. The most important thing to remember is that while your initial response to a stimulus is automatic, you can retrain yourself to respond in a more positive way in the future. This means that an individual's behavior is influenced more by their environment and past experiences than it is innate or inherent. If a child is regularly praised and given a reward for picking up their toys, they will associate those actions with good feelings and be more likely to repeat them in the future. Having learned that meeting deadlines leads to positive outcomes, an employee will be more motivated to do so in the future if they are consistently recognized and rewarded for doing so. A student who is disciplined for disruptive behavior in class may learn from the experience and behave more appropriately in the future. A student's self-defeating belief that any sort of engagement in public can lead to humiliation and rejection may manifest if his punishment is disproportionate to the level of his negative behavior.

Can you see how your experience of life is mostly a result of conscious behavioral choices? What memories and ideas did the last few paragraphs bring to mind?

What behavioral choices did you make in the past that have had a significant impact on your life today?

39

How have your past behavioral choices impacted your relationships with others?

Have your past behavioral choices led to any negative consequences that you are still dealing with today? What are those?

How did the consequences of your past behavioral choices influence your future behavior?

How Have You Learned To Fear Rejection?

Anxiety about being rejected persists long after it first appears, typically in a person's formative years (either in early childhood or adolescence). Because you're highly capable of one-trial learning, you may have developed a strong aversion to opportunities that may result in rejection as a result of the few negative real-life experiences you've had. You can exert more conscious control over your present-day responses by gaining insight into the nature of these experiences from the past.

Is it possible that you sometimes overreact to the words or actions of others, whether they were meant to offend you or you misunderstood them as such? To what extent do you agree or disagree, and what thoughts or recollections did this question bring up?

Your anxiety over being rejected is not coincidental. You've been accumulating memories of physical and emotional pain since you were a young child. The absorption and assembly of these experiences into a survival mechanism provides fertile ground for the development of irrational fears that persist in day to day life. Childhood rejection can happen from anyone in a child's life, including but not limited to parents, teachers, brothers and sisters, cousins, aunts, grandparents, neighbors, and even friends. It might have been intentional or not. In either case, they can color your adult relationships and cause you to reject yourself. Potentially catastrophic defensive reactions could be set off by anything in that virtual memory. Is it fair to say that, now that you're an adult, you find your fear of rejection to be irrational and unwarranted?

What evidence do you have for accepting or rejecting this proposition? How do you feel it manifested in your current reality?

All self-aware humans, regardless of culture or background, share a universal, primal fear of abandonment, and this is a large part of why rejection anxiety is so potent. Because of this, even a single instance of rejection during childhood can spark the development of common survival mechanisms, and one of the most effective methods for a helpless and naive child to ensure his or her own survival is to gain the favor and acceptance of a caregiver. Is there anyone in particular who, as you consider this, you feel responsible for first sparking your fear of rejection?

Do you believe they wanted to harm you at that very moment? How so?

Is it possible that they felt they needed to exert some sort of control over you, and if so, why?

43

Consider your past life experiences and divide your life into seven distinct time frames ("Epochs"). If you are 40 years old, epoch 1 would represent your ages 0 to 6; epoch 2 would represent your ages 7 to 13; and so on. If you are still in your twenties, you might want to divide it into four or five epochs instead of seven.

Today:	Age range	Years
Epoch 1		
Epoch 2		
Epoch 3		
Epoch 4		
Epoch 5		
Epoch 6		
Epoch 7		

Next, take some time to describe three to seven significant events in your life that occurred during each major epoch. What you choose should include both positive and negative experiences.

Select from minor past events, such as the time an attractive stranger smiled at you, as well as from major past events, such as the time you were emotionally hurt, publicly shamed, rejected, or threatened with your safety or wellbeing. There ought to be at least three major events per epoch that make you feel a strong emotion even today when you think back on those incidents.

Title each experience so that you will immediately recognize its meaning if you see it again in the future; this will help you keep track of everything. If you want a more in-depth self-analysis process, you may want to get a copy of Erickson Institute's book - The Big Book of Self-Analysis (ISBN 9788087518120).

EXAMPLE

Epoch 3

Experience	Age / Year	Event Title
A	14 / 2001	John (my brother) makes fun of me in front of my friends for peeing in bed a few nights ago.
B	22/2009	At the corporate meeting, my boss Jen compliments me on my professionalism and good ideas.
C	28/2015	At my high school reunion, the girl I had a crush on in my senior year made fun of me.

All of this is for your eyes only, so be honest and truthful with yourself.

Experience	Age / Year	Event Title
A		
B		
C		
D		
E		
F		
G		

Epoch 2

Experience	Age / Year	Event Title
A		
B		
C		
D		
E		
F		
G		

Experience	Age / Year	Event Title
A		
B		
C		
D		
E		
F		
G		

Epoch 4

Experience

Age / Year	Event Title
A	
B	
C	
D	
E	
F	
G	

Epoch 5

Experience	Age / Year	Event Title
A		
B		
C		
D		
E		
F		
G		

Epoch 6

Experience	Age / Year	Event Title
A		
B		
C		
D		
E		
F		
G		

Experience	Age / Year	Event Title
A		
B		
C		
D		
E		
F		
G		

It's (Kind Of) Your Fault

You are not responsible for the occurrence of the unavoidable events that occur in your life.

You are fully responsible for your reactions to the unavoidable events that occur in your life.

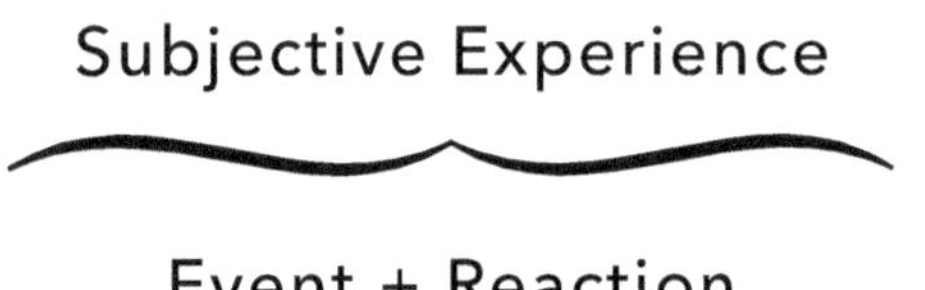

The event (what happens and in what context) and your reaction to it interact to produce your subjective experience, meaning your body-mind state (emotions and thoughts translated as a mood). Your behavioral choices determine how you'll react in any given event or circumstance. Both your conscious and unconscious activities fall into this category. A physical activity could be any behavior involving movement; this includes changes in posture, facial expressions, gestures, etc. Cognitive activities consist of imagination, internal dialogue, and anything within your consciousness. The environment of your consciousness depends on the subject to which your attention is directed at any given moment. The attention can be shifted to whatever you perceive as most pressing at the moment. As a result, you are wholly accountable for the things you choose to focus on and experience, both in the external world and within yourself.

Consider a situation where you acted less effectively than you could have and later wondered, "Why did I do that?!":

You are in charge of your own thoughts and actions because you have the freedom to reevaluate the myriad of options for how to behave. The outcome of the event may remain the same no matter what, but your perception of the here and now will change drastically depending on the response you choose to adopt.

Imagine you and your coworkers are at a party, and someone who has had a few too many starts making jokes about you. When this person sees that your eyes are red and itchy, instead of politely asking if you're experiencing dryness and could use some eye drops, he or she will utter a comment about it and how you look like a vampire. How could you not be offended when the spotlight is shining down on you in such a humiliating way?

The event, on the other hand, is objective reality: someone makes a remark about you in front of everyone. The response you choose to this event will shape your subjective experience of it.Available behavioral choices:

One, act hurt or even cry and tell them they've insulted you, before asking what you did to deserve it.

Two, charge at them, yell angrily, spit out your drink on their pants, punch them in the face, and then storm out the door.

Three, give a half-smile and a wink, and say, "You caught me... "I can't wait to drink your blood tonight..."

Four, take a piece of paper, write down their name, fold it into your pocket, and quietly say, "You're on my blacklist now, buddy; enjoy what little pleasure you have left..."

Five, imitate their actions and expressions in an exaggerated manner, as if they were cartoon characters like Mr. Bean. Play up an obvious flaw in their appearance, like a mole or thinning hair, to impress the audience. And then, because you're having so much fun, ask them to keep going while maintaining your cheerful demeanor.

Six, say calmly and steadily, "So you like making fun of other people's disabilities, huh?"

Seven, wait for the appropriate moment to whisper in their ears, "I recorded the entire thing, and I'm suing you for slender." Sell your home."

Eight, you can put on a bored expression and say flatly, "Once a douche, always a douche... I'm lucky not to be related to you..." and move on to have fun in another corner of the party.

Nine. You can stare at the person and make a silly smile while picturing yourself chopping off their head with a samurai sword. You're completely silent, which may cause them confusion due to the look of happiness on your face.

Ten, as we'll see later, you can instantly change the sub-modalities of what you perceive in the moment and become completely unaffected by other people's intentions to disrupt your enjoyment of the party.

The list goes on and on. We could probably think of a hundred different ways to react, and the vast majority of them wouldn't involve you acting like you'd been kicked in the groin. In fact, right now you might also have a new idea on how you would have reacted differently in this exact situation (come up with at least 3 new potential behavioral choices):

1

2

3

This fundamental concept is the backbone of NLP. The motivation behind an attitude is an essential aspect to consider. The way we feel is something we've thought up on our own; it's not something that has been imposed on us or constructed by someone else. It's a common behavioral practice to fool oneself into thinking that one's own disposition is the consequence of the actions of others, but this is an absurd notion. However, it serves a function in that it excuses us from having to take personal responsibility for our victim mentality, the feelings it evokes, our behavior toward an external stimulus, and the consequences that ensue. What is the more beneficial approach to dealing with current reality? Because you had access to all of these possible behavioral responses, your reaction was -- drum roll please -- your own choice! And the consequences, which manifest almost immediately as emotional and kinesthetic sensations, are entirely your own artificial creation. Would you be willing to spend the rest of your life cuffed in chains to the wall? Of course not. Freedom of cognitive movement is just as crucial. Freedom entails the capacity to choose one's own perspective.

Now, let's talk about the reason you acted the way you did, even though it wasn't the "best" possible behavioral choice you could have made. The reality is that how you reacted was the best behavioral choice you've had available to you in that particular situation and context. That was the quickest mental path your mind could take to react to the situation as it unfolded. The term "path of least resistance" is often used interchangeably with this concept. In other words, you simply didn't know any better. Looking back, we can say, "Oh, right, what I should have done is..." That holds true only in retrospect, not in real time. So, how do you change that habitual way of reacting so you can maintain your freedom and not blame, shame, or guilt yourself later?

Although we can't alter what has already happened, we can improve our odds of facing unpredictable circumstances by making more effective behavioral choices. The key is thus to increase the (beneficial) behavioral choices that may be allowed to become available in current reality.

What past event would win the award of being the most humiliating and painful rejection you've ever experienced? Give it a title:

Date & Time:

Context:

People Involved:

Event (A Brief Objective Description):

Actual Behavioral Choices (Thoughts, Actions):

Alternative Behavioral Choices:

Eventual Outcome:

Potential Outcome:

A few notes on how to complete the table on expansion of behavioral choices:

Your perception of the world is not the same as objective reality ("the map is not the territory"). There is no way that you could ever accurately share your inner life with someone else. Although this is a painful and distressing event, the description should be limited to its objective aspects only. Getting hurt is an effect of the event, not the event itself, as we saw in the preceding example. So instead of writing, "I was humiliated by my boss in front of my co-workers," you ought to write, "The boss made remarks about me in front of the co-workers." The shame or hurt you feel is not caused by the event itself but by how you choose to interpret it.

This is not a creative writing assignment. Keep your responses brief, you can even use one word, as long as you know what it means exactly. Your mind is already aware of the entire story. The goal is to briefly explore alternative routes so that your mind can pick up where you left off and begin coming up with new ideas for similar future situations.

Consider "what I could have done instead" in the "Alternative Behavioral Choices" column on the right rather than "what I should have done."

The word "should" connotes strict discipline, blame, or guilt. The word "could" suggests potential, capability, and learning. We want much less of the former and much more of the latter.

The outcomes are the results of how you processed your perception of the event. Just be honest. What did you choose to keep with you as a result of how you chose to behave? Own the outcome instead of pointing blame where it does not belong. You chose to get hurt, although you did not know better at that moment in time. Lucky Joe, on the other hand, could have ignored the attempts of others to hurt his feelings and instead used the situation to experience a good laugh or gain new insights and knowledge. Subsequent chapters will go into greater detail on additional methods for accomplishing this.

The eventual outcome could be, "I feel hurt when I think about it, and I wonder why anyone would do this to a nice guy like me?! The potential outcome could be, "I learned who my true friends are; what a relief! I can now say no to Jeff without fear of losing a friend."

To help you explore other painful memories, we've included a few more copies of this form at the end of this book.

Quit the Blame Game

When you're experiencing fear of rejection, it's sometimes (or perhaps quite often) a sign that you're taking things personally and inappropriately. The reason is deeper and more universal than you think.

How do you typically react when something negative happens or when you face a challenge?

Do you tend to first blame yourself or first look for external causes for negative events or problems? Do you typically look within yourself or outside yourself for answers to why bad things keep happening? Do you usually look for internal or external causes?

Fear of rejection can lead us to falsely blame ourselves in an attempt to avoid social rejection. This is because we may believe that if we find the "problem" that is causing the rejection, we can eliminate it and never experience rejection again. Self-blame can give us the illusion that we are in charge of the situation and can take steps to prevent further rejection and, by doing so, deal with our anxious expectations of a painful future. This way of thinking, however, is frequently flawed because it causes us to take the blame for events that are not in our sphere of influence. For example, we may blame ourselves for someone else's negative behavior or for events that are not related to us at all. Because of this, you may find it hard to break the pattern of needlessly antagonizing and doubting yourself. Moreover, our sense of value and competence can suffer as a result of this misguided effort to avoid being rejected.

What patterns have you noticed in the types of things you tend to blame yourself for?

How do you determine whether something is directly your fault or not? Do you believe your gut instinct, or do you first hear a voice in your head talking to you (2nd person) instead of being you (1st person) - "Look at you, dufus!" vs. "I'm such a slob..."? Any specific mental images come to mind when you blame your self for someone else's actions or words?

Repeatedly placing the blame on one's own shoulders can result in a detrimental belief system in which you begin to feel directly to blame for all of life's misfortunes. This in turn continues the loop by resulting in a negative self-perception and a lack of confidence in our abilities.

Do you have a hard time accepting credit where credit is due or letting go of liability and blame when it is not your fault? How does this problem impact your day-to-day life?

It is natural for us to see ourselves as the center of everything when we are young. Because our experiences and perspectives as children are limited to our own thoughts and actions, it is natural for us to regard ourselves as the most important person in our world. However, as we grow and develop, we become aware that there is a much larger world out there beyond our own experiences. We discover that others have their own thoughts, feelings, and desires, and that the world does not revolve entirely around us.

This realization can be liberating as well as disheartening. On the one hand, it enables us to see ourselves in relation to the larger world and comprehend our place within it. On the other hand, it can make us feel insignificant and small in the grand scheme of things. While it is true that we are not the center of the universe, it is also true that we are important and have the ability to make a difference in the world. You may not be the most important person in the universe, but you are still significant for the mere reason that you are here, existing for a minuscule portion of time.

It is critical to maintain a sense of humility as we grow and develop and to remember that we are part of a larger whole. We must strive to see the world through the eyes of others and recognize that our actions and decisions have an impact on those around us. Finally, understanding that we are not the focal point of the universe can help us become better, more empathetic, and more understanding people. Understanding our place in the world and developing empathy for others are facilitated by expanding our perspective beyond our inner world.

Do you feel like you have to take on more personal accountability than is reasonable or fair? Do you get the sense that you tend to do so often only to avoid being scrutinized or criticized?

When we take things personally, we frequently expect others to blame us for any negative events or interactions. This expectation can be caused by a number of factors, such as low self-esteem, a negative self-image, or a history of being criticized or blamed by others. If someone makes a remark that we take to be critical or argumentative, we may react defensively, as though they are placing the blame on us. This expectation of blame can make us feel vulnerable and anxious, and it may cause us to avoid certain situations or interactions because we are afraid of being targeted or rejected.

A person's physical and emotional states can change when they blame themselves for things that are not in their control. Here are some examples of common bodily experiences:

• Muscle tension or tightness, most commonly in the upper back, shoulders, and neck

• Irregular or excessively fast heartbeat

• Shortness of breath or difficulty breathing

• Nausea or abdominal pain

• Headache

• Dry mouth or difficulty swallowing

And we can certainly experience a wide range of unpleasant emotions:

• Guilt

• Shame

• Anxiety

• Depression

• Anger

• Frustration

What emotions do you experience when you blame yourself for things that are not under your direct and full control? How does it feel kinesthetically in your body? Where do you feel tightness or pain? What thoughts and beliefs accompany that physical sensation? In other words, what's it like to beat yourself up over circumstances that aren't your fault?

A person's inability to trust others and lack of social connections may begin with a fear of rejection and spiral out of control from there. If you're afraid of being rejected, you might be less likely to trust others because you think they won't treat you fairly if you do. Negative coping mechanisms, such as withdrawing from social situations, becoming overly critical of others, or engaging in dishonest behavior, can emerge in response to this anxiety. Those who are sensitive to the possibility of being rejected may withdraw from social situations that could lead to rejection, such as committed relationships or the revealing of personal information. In addition, they may be more likely to misinterpret the motives of others or to doubt the reliability of others despite evidence to the contrary.

How do you typically cope when you are facing criticism or blame from others? Do you have a tendency to internalize negative feedback or criticism from others, even if it is excessive?

Do you have trouble trusting others? In what ways? In which contexts? Is it limited to specific people or to every person you come in contact with?

Some people worry that if they fail at something, others will dislike or reject them, and this type of anxiety is frequently associated with a fear of failure. By placing the blame on yourself, you are giving yourself the opportunity to initiate the hurtful feelings ahead of time (predicting the unknown future) rather than taking a chance and perhaps experiencing them in real time, and all of that in an effort to avoid the potential negative outcomes in the future. As a result, you stop trying new things or taking risks because you "feel" the pain that is probably going to come and decide it's not worth it. The fallout of this flawed mode of reasoning includes procrastination, perfectionism, people-pleasing, and a general unwillingness to stand out.

How do you feel about failing, making crucial mistakes, or running into problems that are too complicated for you to solve?

Your feelings can be hurt regardless of whether or not the behavior or gesture was intended to do so. If this happens to you frequently and involves people you need to be able to respect, you may start to think there's something fundamentally wrong with you. It's not easy to alter the firm doctrines you've formed about who you are. It's possible that you're only open to hearing the kinds of feedback that reinforce the negative perceptions you hold about yourself. You could indeed ignore any praise that comes your way because it contradicts your subjective reality (mental maps). Take a moment to consider this. When was the last time you were so confused by a compliment because it was so at odds with your negative self-perception that you literally couldn't take it in? Did you have a similar thought to "If they only knew who I really am, they wouldn't ever consider thinking I'm so great"?

Do you have a hard time accepting that sometimes things just happen and are not anyone's fault, not even your own? In what context do you find yourself struggling with these thoughts and feelings?

Let yourself reflect on a time when you felt emotionally hurt because of someone else's rejection. This could be a rejection in a romantic relationship, a job interview that went sour, or anything else that made you feel unwanted or undesirable. Describe the situation in detail —what did you see, hear, and feel immediately before, during, and after it ended?

How is the simple reality that you are hurt because of someone else's fault? What were their malicious intentions in so harshly rejecting you? What if they had rejected you with some grace and spared you the pain? How could they have done so? Did they say there was something fundamentally wrong with you that was the reason they didn't accept you?

What part of this situation is your fault? What errors in judgment did you have to commit in order to find yourself in this situation and in such an inferior position?

This is how you chose to engage in the blame game. Because you make the conscious decision to participate in this game, you can retrain your mind to instead engage in a better and more beneficial game: "the compassion game."

The following NLP script is intended to aid in accessing the unconscious and guiding it to weaken the habitual blame game neurological links and create new ones that would lead you to become curious about learning from current reality and eventually feel self-compassion when faced with potential rejection. Use the script on a regular basis, as often as it feels comfortable and beneficial to you. The script's imagery and suggestions were designed to re-shape your thoughts and potential behavioral choices in more positive and helpful ways over time. All the intentional cognitive work you've been doing so far is being reinforced by using this script.

Make a recording of the script with your own voice. This may have a greater impact and feel more personal than listening to someone else's voice. To record the script, you can use a phone app, a computer program, or simply a voice recorder. Dedicate some uninterrupted time to hearing the script. It is generally best to listen to the script first thing in the morning and again before falling asleep. This allows the symbolism and suggestions to penetrate deeper into your unconscious mind. Get into a cozy position, either sitting or lying down, and make sure you won't be disturbed while reading the script. To help you relax, close your eyes and take a few deep breaths.

Begin by listening to the script and following along as closely as possible with the imagery and ideas. As a result, it's critical to try to visualize as many details of the scenes and events described in the script as possible. Allow yourself to become completely immersed in the script and imagery. It is normal to have thoughts or distractions during the process; however, try to ignore them and return your attention to the scene. When you've listening to the recording, take a few deep breaths and slowly open your eyes. Take a moment to reflect on any feelings or insights that have arisen during the process. Writing down your thoughts or meditating on them can help you make sense of your experience. One NLP script should be used every day, and it is strongly advised to use it consistently for a total of 30 days in a row.

The recommended time between scripts is three days to allow your unconscious mind to purge old ideas and form new ones. You will notice this happening when your early morning dreams become more nebulous and realistic, such as when you dream of real people from your past who don't belong in the context of the dream. Recently, a client shared with us (and gave us permission to share) his recurring dream about his high school teacher bouncing on a trampoline in his parents' living room while his mother tries to convince her to take a break and eat some of his favorite soup.

The unconscious mind is thought to play a role in processing and organizing information that we have encountered during the day, as well as in maintaining important memories and regulating our physical and emotional well-being. One way that the unconscious mind may do this is through the use of early morning dreams, which are thought to be a means of communicating with the conscious mind and may serve as a way to process unconscious materials that were once useful but no longer are. These dreams can serve as a way for the unconscious mind to work through old, limiting ideas and resolve conflicts or emotional issues. Early morning dreams tend to be more vivid and memorable than dreams that occur earlier in the sleep cycle. It is important to note that the interpretation of dreams is a highly personal and subjective experience, and there is no one-size-fits-all explanation for the meanings of dreams. Some people find it helpful to reflect on their dreams and consider what they might be trying to tell them, while others prefer not to think about their dreams at all. We don't even attempt to interpret dreams in our therapeutic model, especially early morning dreams, as we only take them as a sign of progress in therapy.

Day	Date	Insights / Early Morning Dreams
1		
2		
3		
4		
5		
6		
7		
8		
9		
10		

Day	Date	Insights / Early Morning Dreams
11		
12		
13		
14		
15		
16		
17		
18		
19		
20		

Day	Date	Insights / Early Morning Dreams
21		
22		
23		
24		
25		
26		
27		
28		
29		
30		

When You Fail Before You Even Try: a Paralyzing Fear of Rejection

Fear of rejection can certainly paralyze a person's ability to capitalize on current reality's opportunities. The inability to take the next step in pursuing a romantic relationship or even to express interest in another person is one symptom of this paralysis. It's possible that they're paralyzed by anxiety about the potential consequences of taking action, such as being rejected or deemed inadequate by the other person. This incapacity for action can also manifest as professional stagnation. As an illustration, they may be reluctant to offer up their eligibility for a new position or speak up for a raise because they fear being turned down. Because of this apprehension, they may avoid taking on additional responsibilities or expanding their professional range of possibilities. Even pro athletes aren't immune. In sports, this type of paralysis can cause a person to hold back or not perform to their full potential. They may play tentatively or avoid taking risks because they are afraid of making mistakes and being judged negatively by their teammates, coaches, or fans.

Fear of rejection can be crippling, and it often manifests itself through the recognition of sensory stimuli that are associated with long-buried memories of being rejected. These memories may include experiences of being rejected by others, such as being rejected by a romantic partner or being excluded by peers. Various sensory cues, such as hints of the original experience of rejection through sight, sound, smell, taste, or touch, can resurrect these flashbacks.

A person with a fear of rejection, for instance, might have a strong emotional reaction when they see someone who looks like a former potential romantic partner who rejected them. This could be because the person's brain has learned to automatically associate the person's sight with painful past negative rejection.

Similarly, hearing a song that was playing during a time when they were rejected by someone, or its aftermath while trying to get over it, may evoke strong emotions in a person who has insecurities. Some people's brains are hardwired to automatically associate the sound of a certain song with painful memories of past defeat.

Sensory stimuli such as sights, sounds, smells, tastes, and touches can all trigger memories of rejection. Those who are sensitive to rejection, for instance, may have a strong reaction to the scent of the perfume or cologne once worn by the person who rejected them. A person's brain may, on an unconscious level, associate the scent of the perfume or cologne with the painful rejection they experienced.

It is important to recognize that these sensory stimuli are not the cause of the fear of rejection. Rather, they are merely reminders of the past that prompt the recall of uncomfortable or unpleasant emotional reactions. However, being aware of these sensory cues can be a significant step toward comprehending and overcoming rejection anxiety. A person can learn to manage their emotional reactions to rejection by becoming aware of the sensory cues that bring back painful memories.

There is a time lag, a gap, between when you consciously or unconsciously recognize a significant sensory stimulus, such as seeing the blonde hair of a tall guy or hearing the exact type of laughter your memory is associated with, and when you experience rejection anxiety in your body. That gap is where you make a behavioral choice, albeit mostly habitually, to bring up old memories that you have worked so hard to forget. The real reason you find it so easy to make yourself miserable in the present is that you haven't dealt effectively enough with these upsetting memories. Nothing is worse for the human psyche than mental boredom and emptiness. Our brains are constantly scanning for information that could indicate how we are doing and whether or not we are in danger. Our minds excel at recognizing sensory input cues that were previously associated with intense emotions. In the following chapters, we'll learn how to undo these neurological associations between innocent current reality cues (the tall, blonde guy or the woman laughing have nothing to do with your past) and emotional distress and, therefore, regain control over what happens in that gap between awareness and reaction.

To do so effectively, however, we must first identify as many triggers as possible.

On the following page, you'll find an event tracking table (we've added additional copies of this form for your convenience at the end of this book). During the course of the week, take note of the circumstances under which you experience rejection anxiety. Whether it's something you see, hear, feel (in your body, on your skin), smell, or taste, make a note of the sensations that stand out as being distinctive. Make connections between your immediate sensory experience and the thoughts that occur to you. A word of caution, though: if you're feeling particularly down that day, it's best not to engage in this process or look for external cues lest your brain create illegitimate associations where none existed before. If you're having a good day and then all of a sudden you feel anxious and vividly recall a troubling memory of rejection, it can help to get curious and use your physical senses to figure out what triggered those thoughts and emotions. Ensure that you document your discovery as soon as possible.

You might find that doing this regularly, along with some of the other tools in this book, helps you get a better handle on your automatic panic response, which shows up as rejection anxiety.

Day / Time	I Felt / Thought…	Perhaps because of…

Day / Time	I Felt / Thought...	Perhaps because of...

Soothing Emotional Scars

Someone must have told you, "It's been so long since then; forget about it; the past is the past," at some point in your life. A painful emotional experience is not easily forgotten. In our work, we often encounter clients in their 50s and 60s who are still struggling with the emotional wounds they sustained as adolescents. Emotional scars are so-called because they contaminate your mind with limiting beliefs and misguided "truisms" about your true nature, potential, and self-worth. You may know intellectually that you are a valuable human being, but if a single insult, nick name, or threatening gesture can send you spiraling into feelings of worthlessness, the blame lies with the emotional scars you have carried with you for years, or even decades. The scars are invisible until you encounter a reminder in real life.

The memories and the agony they bring can seem to arise out of nowhere and overwhelm your consciousness. Feelings of embarrassment, remorse, and pain consume you, and you can't stop thinking about the person who hurt you, the words or actions that were used, and the alternative actions you might have taken.

In addition, your mind is conditioned to use the emotionally charged recollections of these past events as a significant factor in your decision-making because ruminating over them feels familiar and known. It develops into an unconscious method of coping with stress. It reduces the threat of the unknown future by comparing incoming stimuli to significant past experiences. This is a survival strategy. Your mind labels as harmful, dangerous, and off-limits anything that resembles, even in the slightest bit, what caused you suffering in the past.

We'll be dealing with these emotional scars in stages. Our topmost priority right now is to cut down as quickly as possible on the effect that they are having on the state of your body and mind in the here and now. We accomplish this by gradually training your mind to gain control over how these memories are activated and processed in your consciousness. Note that we do not change or distort the content of your memories in any way. We accept your recollection of the event as it has transpired thus far in your imagination without alteration of the words or actions. We do not argue against, rationalize, or try to decipher the meaning of what has happened to you. We only pay attention to the syntax and form involved in enacting that memory in the here and now. Attempting to alter the information of past experiences is a dangerous game of wishful thinking that yields only short-term relief and encourages escape.

Fear of rejection is how you learned to protect yourself as a defenseless and innocent young child. This is not a psychological malfunction. In the grand scheme of things, this survival mechanism has been essential. When you accept that your insecurities, fears, and self-imposed limitations are merely adaptations rather than pathologies, you can begin to treat your mind as the miraculous creation that it is. Your sensitive mind had to quickly ramp up its defenses in order to survive during your formidable years, and the resulting grandiose and fierce adaptation has solidified into a neurobiological process you now call rejection anxiety.

Worrying that you will be abandoned, or even worse, denied access to basic needs like shelter, food, protection, and affection, can cause a child to develop a crippling fear of rejection. Whether it was your parents, older siblings, or other close friends and neighbors, you needed to not only fit in but also be accepted by those you viewed as more powerful than you. Being isolated from these evolving social networks poses serious risks. Our minds did not yet evolve to take for granted all the convenience and security we enjoy in the modern era, so this is a holdover from the brains of our ancestors. When we are young, our behavior is governed primarily by the primitive animal instincts stored in our brains. All the conveniences we come to rely on as adults are the result of the ego's training to expect them.

Consider the earliest time you remember feeling rejected or afraid of potential rejection. What about that era, that setting, and those people that gave the impression of heightened vulnerability (to a naive and impressionable child)?

How did fitting in, not speaking up, not asking for what you knew you wouldn't get, and keeping your head down protect you from harm at that time and in that place?

Can you look back as an adult, no longer a defenseless child, and appreciate your adaptation to a harsh reality?

Can you admit that as a child you had very limited access to information about the world, your civil rights (to be fed, protected, and educated), your options (to stay, to leave, to demand respect), and so on?

Your brain had to develop an extreme response to a very powerful and potentially harmful stimulus because you lacked the adequate resources to deal with it in the way that you would be able to today. Can you accept that vulnerability as it is and not argue against it? Can you admit that, yes, it served you well when it was most needed, but now that you've grown and matured, you're ready to let it go, both with gratitude for the role it played in your life and without frustration for the consequences it has had on your present life?

Let's get past the deductive reasoning and begin retraining your nervous system to more efficiently process your memories. Once more, we will not alter the content of the memories directly. We won't try to decipher them or figure out what led to the initial event that occurred. It is important to remember that the actual event has concluded, whether it was last week or 50 years ago, and has no real affect on the world that surrounds you at this time. We've already established that it's not the content of the memory itself that matters, but rather how you process it in the present, as evidenced by the fact that two people can recall a very similar or even shared experience and derive very different reactions to that memory.

Since people are creatures of habit, their negative responses to remembering an emotionally charged past event become systematic and repetitive. The more you access that memory using the same sequence of representational systems and their driving sub-modalities, the stronger the neurological link between the idea to recall the memory and the kinesthetic (physiological) response that is translated back as a specific emotion (anxiety, sadness, regret, etc.).

Now perform a quick calculation. Is there a monthly, weekly, or daily average for how often you think back on the one particularly unpleasant memory? How much time has passed since the real-world event concluded? Could it be that you mentally replayed that memory more than a hundred times? Thousands of times?

Because of the chemical nature of emotions, every time you practiced this, you experienced a wave of physical discomfort. And by repeating this pattern, you have taught your brain to react strongly whenever you think about or recall that particular memory. Meanwhile, another person (lucky Joe) who went through the same thing you did reacted differently, perhaps even more effectively, and so that memory does not hunt his conscious attention in the same way it does for you. Lucky Joe did not bother recalling the event hundreds or thousands of times. Lucky Joe's mind deemed that memory less important and as boring as thinking about umbrellas as a result of the behavioral choice to shrug it off.

Again, like we mentioned earlier, the only difference between you and that lucky Joe is in how you access the recall in current reality. It's in the syntax and form of activating the representational systems and their driving sub-modalities. It is a boring memory for lucky Joe because in his mind, the mental movie is not impressive at all, in terms of representational systems.

It's the same feeling you get when you go to the movies. Let's say you're sitting alone in an empty theater with no one around. Even though it's a large-screen presentation, the film only fills up half of the screen, and you notice how silly and unprofessional it looks. The projector also seems to be broken, as it switches to black and white, the pictures on the screen are out of focus and the running images loses sync with the sound at random. As if that weren't bad enough, the speakers are making a scratchy, disturbing noise. Still, that's not the worst of it; the rigidity of your seat makes it difficult to relax and follow the action on screen. What would it be like for you to watch that movie? Most likely, your first reaction would be, "What are you talking about?" "I couldn't even watch it!" That has nothing to do with the film's plot, which hasn't changed. It is due to the form and syntax of watching that film.

Theater one:

In order to fully appreciate a movie while watching it in a theater, every aspect of the processing needs to run smoothly. The movie is being displayed in its entirety on the big screen. The sound is synchronized, very clear, and very loud from the speakers. Your seat is cozy, and you experience all the feelings the filmmaker intended. You thrill at the action sequences, cry at the unexpected deaths of beloved characters, and flinch in your seat at the sight of violent assault. You chose to participate in that film and invest emotionally, didn't you? Compare the first theater experience to the second.

Theater two:

The same thing happens inside your mental theater at all hours of the day and night. You create mental movies and conduct inner conversations that direct your subjective experience. You are constantly switching between the roles of the script writer, director, casting agent, props supervisor, camera man and lead actor in your mental movies.

And what about lucky Joe? To him, it's like watching that first movie in the theater when he recalls the same traumatic event that's bothering you. It's all scratchy and impossible to watch or participate in. So it's no wonder his mind finds it dull and unimpressive. Cognitively, he has a much more difficult time recalling that memory, and thus his access to the memory contains a fraction of the neurological connections that yours does.

On the other hand, you are so immersed in that memory that you experience it all over again, just like in the second theater scenario. It's 3D, it's big, it's impressive, and you feel like you're actually a part of the scene. You would naturally feel some level of excitement, anxiety, etc. You feel as though you've been transported into the scene and are participating in the subjective experience as though it were literally taking place in the real world at this very moment. The most important clue is that it exists only in your head. The real event has long been concluded. It's possible that it will never happen again in the real world. It will always contain the same plot because you can't alter the past. The question is, how can you adjust your response to it? You guessed it—make a behavioral choice and move to the other theater! And that's what sub-modalities can do for you.

The moving pictures (visual representational system) associated with a particularly powerful and vivid memory tend to fill the entire screen whenever that memory is retrieved. That's why, even if you've thought about a certain memory many times before, you can still get caught up in the experience. Add to that the auditory representational system, which contains sounds and speech that come at you as if your mind has a high-end home theater with surround sound, loud and clear enough to grab your attention right away. All of this then elicits bodily sensations (the kinesthetic representational system) and makes you feel like you're reliving the original experience, albeit with a notable difference: you are also aware that you aren't actually there, and so your reactions are somewhat milder than they could be in a real-life event.

The physiological effect, though, is still significant. Because of this vivid representation, your unconscious mind believes it is a real event taking place in real time. Hormones are activated, and their chemical signals flow through your body. While there is no tiger in the bushes—and perhaps no bushes at all—your whole system reacts as if that beast is just about to eat you alive at any second. Estimate how often you've relived this mental series of images from a disturbing memory. You have "earned" the physiological stress responses by practicing what eventually activates these stress hormones; if you knew this, you would understand why fear of rejection is sabotaging your purest intentions; why you may have, or soon will have, stress-related diseases (high cholesterol, high blood pressure, joint pain, ED, carpal tunnel syndrome, and so many more); and why challenges in your life seem to just pop up in a vicious cycle that never seems to be resolved. Same old, same old.

Lucky Joe's mind, on the other hand, used a different form and syntax to access a similar memory. The internal representation he had was fuzzy, difficult to interpret, and distorted. As a result, it has left no imprint on lucky Joe's unconscious mind, much like a random thought about umbrellas. There was no release of stress hormones or other physiological responses, and there were no adverse effects, either short- or long-term, on the body. We emphasize this crucial point because it bears repeating: your reaction to a past event that is no longer taking place has nothing to do with the content of that memory. It all depends on how you choose to access (syntax) and process (form) that memory.

Spend the next few minutes thinking about and writing freely about this: What would happen to you if, like Lucky Joe, your disturbing memories played out in your mind like a movie in a theater? How would it feel like?

What if all of your wonderful and enlivening memories were played out in your mind as a movie in theater two?

Assuming you were able to manage both: bad memories are vague and good memories are vivid, how would you normally spend your days?

What thought would never enter your mind ever again? What would you notice around you, in terms of sights, sounds, other people's reactions to you?

Now for the meat of the challenge: which upsetting memories would you rather retain as guardrails to prevent you from falling into the same traps again? One such memory might involve a slick street vendor who pressured you into buying an expensive item you did not need. Even if remembering the experience makes you feel humiliated or embarrassed, it may be useful to hold on to the memory so that you can use it as a warning system the next time you're faced with a similar situation.

What follows can be done with or without your eyes closed, though closing them may be more practical and convenient. What you "see" in your mind when you close your eyes is a three-dimensional representation of anything that could potentially enter your realm of consciousness. If you don't have anything going on cognitively, the mental screen may appear black. That mental projection screen could look something like this, spanning across your entire field of (internal) vision:

Internal experiences can be classified as either associated or dissociated. Knowing the distinctions and differences between the two is crucial. When you see, hear, and sense the mental event in the first person, you are associated with it. You get to experience the scene as if you were there yourself, going through the motions. You are living or reliving your fantasy. Obviously, the peak of the associated experience is when one feels the most intense emotions and sensations.

Dissociation is defined as viewing an experience from a distance while remaining uninvolved in the imagined event. You're assuming the perspective of a fly on the wall. You are observing the scene in your mind and creating a mental movie of it, but you are not actively participating. Being removed from the action naturally dampens the intensity of the experience.

Association and dissociation are both behavioral choices. Because the mental movie is playing inside your own mind, you have the option of being immersed in it (associated) or simply observing it from a safe distance (dissociated).

If you close your eyes and imagine yourself reading a book, this illustrated point of view would be the fully associated experience (seeing the book and your hands through your own eyes):

A dissociated experience, on the other hand, is when you take the point of view of a bystander or an observer. You see your own image there on the screen, as if it's a home movie of sort, in which you can see your face and body on the screen:

Let's try it with your own memories now. Think back on an enjoyable experience you had in the past. Any of the pleasant memories you've discovered throughout your epochs will do, but you're free to pick another if you prefer. Describe this memory in general:

Try closing your eyes and imagining yourself back in the time and place of this personal memory. Imagine yourself back in that moment, reliving it in all its sensory detail. Here, you play the lead role and observe events as they unfold firsthand.

After that, return to the beginning of the mental movie and make the image brighter and the sounds and voices louder and closer to you. The image and sounds should be slightly brighter and louder at each stage of the experience. Is it more enjoyable / exciting than the first time you imagined the movie?

Most people, depending on the context, find that increasing the brightness of their mental image or the volume of the sounds they hear increases the intensity of their kinesthetic responses. Put another way, the intensity of your emotional reaction to a mental image increases as its brightness increases. This bodily sensation also convinces us that the mental movie is either factual or extremely believable. That's the kind (form and syntax) of thinking that can lead to panic attacks, a skewed chemical balance, and other unpleasant emotions.

The reason for this is that this is exactly what you do with limiting beliefs, traumatic memories, and insecurities: you create mental movies that represent these notions in a form that is bright and big and loud and impressive, so the critical thinking parts of your brain believe it to be true and make choices based on that perspective. Most people do not use their brains in an appropriate or deliberate manner. They let their thoughts wander down well-worn but inefficient routes without stopping to consider that they were the ones who made the choice. Now think of lucky Joe. When confronted with the mental movie, he consciously chose a different path to take, and that behavioral choice resulted in a predictable outcome: the memory of a horrible past event does not bother him at all.

Can you see how it all comes back to you making a specific sequence of behavioral choices and ending up feeling fearful of rejection when it is least appropriate or needed?

Now let's take it a step further.

Simply recall the same pleasant memory as before and turn the brightness down—just dim the lights about 50%. Reduce the volume of the voices and sounds you hear, so they're a bit harder to understand. How does this version of the movie stack up against your previous mental image (with the lights turned up and the volume turned up)? Is it more or less enjoyable / exciting than the previous time you imagined the movie (with the brightness up and louder sound)?

Last but not least, increase the brightness and volume levels back up to where they were when you first recalled this pleasant memory. Since this is a happy memory, we don't want to dampen your spontaneous response to it.

Brightness and volume are just two examples of sub-modalities in their respective visual and auditory representational systems. There are many more sub-modalities to explore and investigate, and focusing on the ones that are most influential for you (what we call driving sub-modalities) will yield the most immediate and impressive results.

A change in behavior would necessitate the acquisition of a new learned response to replace the old one. Just gaining knowledge is not enough. This suggests that the strategy by which the new pattern will be established must be identical to the one that the learned pattern will replace. For illustration, consider a memory that keeps coming back to you, even though it makes you feel dreadful. Relive the experience by visualizing and reacting to the events as they unfolded. Except in extreme cases like an accident, where dissociation is a natural defense mechanism, memories do not incorporate seeing oneself in the event. You should be sure that this memory truly does hurt your feelings. Knowing it makes you feel horrible, run the memory forward, and as soon as you reach the end, run it fast backward to the beginning. Do that five times in a row. Now, within 3 seconds, fast-forward the mental movie from beginning to end and then rewind rapidly backward to the beginning. Repeat that sequence five times.

What you've done is alter two driving sub-modalities of the visual representational system: speed and direction. Now, take a few moments to reflect on the experience and determine whether it still makes you feel the way it did just before:

One approach to lessening the impact of a negative memory is to recall it in reverse order. The content is the same, but the syntax is used differently by re-sequencing the mental representations. Rather than letting the process take its habitual course, you can take charge (and thus responsibility) by altering the activation in the present moment, which is what we mean when we talk about lessening emotional scars. You cannot alter the original memory by disputing or bargaining with it. What you do fully know, however, is that what you think you endured in the original event is dependent on your own limited perspective; this is because your subjective experience is the only way you get to live life. The things that were said or done to you or by you would have remained the same even if you assumed a different perspective right afterward. Because you could have chosen a different perspective during the original event, the perspective you chose is not a consequence of the event itself. It is not part of the event's content. So, you see where this is going, right? Just because you had that perspective back then doesn't mean you can't have a different perspective on the same event today. Because perspective exists only in your mind, you have complete control over what happens there, regardless of what happens outside of your body. Even years after the fact, your memory of an event can be profoundly altered by shifting your perspective. That is, you feel differently about it, and hopefully you learn and adapt in a healthy and effective way that will benefit you in your current reality and in the future.

Do you understand the significance of this phenomenon? Can you see that, because of your newfound awareness, this mental procedure no longer needs to be automatic if you so choose? How might you benefit from it as you consider pursuing your desires?

You have experimented shortly with a few sub-modalities: brightness, loudness, speed and direction. There are many more you may want to play with. As you may have noticed, the sub-modalities distinctions are important because they alter how we experience our thoughts. They determine whether we get excited or bored, motivated or anxious. The more you understand about the driving sub-modalities that code your unique mind's translation of your current reality experience, the more control you have over how you live your life.

Here are all of the main sub-modalities of the visual representational system:

Motion:

Is it a movie or a still photograph?

Color:

Is it in color or black and white? How bright are the colors? Is there a dominant color that stands out? Is the picture tinted with a particular filter (say, a vintage filter)?

Size:

How big is the image, relatively? Do you have to move your head up to see more of it? Are you aware of elements that are not in direct view due to its size? Is it too small to notice any specific details?

Dimension:

Is the image flat (2D) or three-dimensional (3D)? Does it cover your entire field of vision (wrapped around you in all directions) or is it like a flat screen in front of you? Does it look more like a home made movie or a stop motion or even a cartoon?

Spatial location:

What is the exact location of the image? More to the left or right, up or down? How would you "hold" the image if you were asked to do so with your hands? Does it "hang" towards one side as if it's magnetically attached?

Proportions:

Is everything in the picture about the same size as it would be in real life, or are some of the people or objects disproportionately large or small?

Brightness:

Is it brighter or darker than normal in that context?

Contrast:

Is there a lot of contrast, or is it damp?

Distance:

How far away from your face is the image?

Texture:

What kind of texture does the picture have, smooth or rough?

Focus:

Is the image in focus or out of focus? If it is out of focus, to what degree?

Visual Data:

Does it have both foreground and background elements? Can you take in the whole picture while still recognizing the smaller parts? Do the specifics jump out at you or do you have to shift your attention to take them in?

Global shape:

Does the image have a specific form, such as a square, an oval, a rectangle (16:9), etc.?

Frame:

Is the image framed? Does it have a defined edge, or do the corners blur out? What color is the border, if any? What's the thickness of the border?

Overall external movement:

Does the image tremble or wobble, or is it solid and steady? So, if the image is shaky, to which direction does it move most heavily?

Speed of thought:

If this is a mental film, how fast does it play? Is it faster than normal? Does the movie omit moments from the real event?

Orientation:

is the image tilted in any direction?

Perceptual Position:

Is it associated or dissociated? Can you see your whole self in the image, or do you experience the memory through your own eyes as if you're there again?What point of view is it if it is dissociated?

Perspective:

Where do you, the spectator, stand in relation to the action if the image is disassociated? What is the distance and proximity to the screen? From which direction? Do you recognize yourself in the picture from different angles? Do you see yourself in that image from the front, side, or back? From above, in a bird's-eye view? Or as if you (the observer) were peering over your (self) movie character's shoulder?

Variety:

Does the mental event project one or more images to represent it? If there is more than one, what is the difference between them in terms of your perspective? Do you see different images depending on your vantage point? Are the multiple images arriving simultaneously or in sequence (as in, seeing the event from one direction and then another)? Do you make use of the multiple concurrent images to evaluate different options?

What does it feel like to envision your future as ambiguous, distorted, framed in metal bars, dark, and murky? These are the sub-modalities at play when anxiety is induced by the mind.

Some people use this frame of mind as the primary strategy to perceive and then translate the meaning of their current reality. How ineffective and distressful is that approach, anyway?

Try thinking back on a positive, fun and highly enjoyable event that happened to you not too long ago:

The original event's intention, time, place, circumstance, and participants are all components of its context. Even if the time and place are identical, the vibe of recalling a romantic dinner with your significant other is very different from that of a family dinner. The reason the vibe is different is due to shifts in visual sub-modalities.

The sub-modalities of this memory can be evaluated with the help of the following table. In the left column, circle the characteristic that stands out to you visually. This could be whether it is a movie or a photograph, whether it is moving slowly or quickly, etc. On the right column select how intensely that attribute is when you normally recall that memory. The only thing that the intensity level refers to is how powerful or impressive that particular aspect of the memory is. Because it is not an exact science, you should rely on your intuition and make an educated guess.

You can make it simpler for yourself by opening your eyes after each sub-modality evaluation and taking a moment to look at the environment around you. When you temporarily remove yourself from your thoughts in order to get back in touch with the world around you, we refer to this as a "break state." As a side note, if you find yourself in a mind-body state that is less than optimal, such as lethargy, excessive worrying, or getting caught up in endless mind chatter, you may want to consider breaking state to gain back control . You can break state by physically acting in a way that differs from your usual patterns of behavior, such as making a behavioral choice that is completely unrelated to the situation at hand. For instance, making a funny face, beatboxing, coughing out loud, stretching while singing "Stayin' Alive," handstands, and bouncing up and down.

Visual Sub-modalities Elicitation

Intensity

▷ Movie   ▷ Still Image   ① ② ③ ④ ⑤ ⑥ ⑦ ⑧ ⑨

▷ Associated   ▷ Dissociated   ① ② ③ ④ ⑤ ⑥ ⑦ ⑧ ⑨

▷ Color   ▷ Black & White   ① ② ③ ④ ⑤ ⑥ ⑦ ⑧ ⑨

▷ Location: ↑ → ↓ ←   ① ② ③ ④ ⑤ ⑥ ⑦ ⑧ ⑨

▷ Distance: Close   ▷ Distance: Far   ① ② ③ ④ ⑤ ⑥ ⑦ ⑧ ⑨

▷ Light: Dim   ▷ Light: Bright   ① ② ③ ④ ⑤ ⑥ ⑦ ⑧ ⑨

▷ Contrast: Vibrant   ▷ Contrast: Damp   ① ② ③ ④ ⑤ ⑥ ⑦ ⑧ ⑨

▷ Size: Small   ▷ Size: Large   ① ② ③ ④ ⑤ ⑥ ⑦ ⑧ ⑨

▷ Focus: Sharp   ▷ Focus: Blurr   ① ② ③ ④ ⑤ ⑥ ⑦ ⑧ ⑨

▷ Speed: Slow   ▷ Speed: Fast   ① ② ③ ④ ⑤ ⑥ ⑦ ⑧ ⑨

▷ Panoramic   ▷ Framed   ① ② ③ ④ ⑤ ⑥ ⑦ ⑧ ⑨

▷ Texture: Smooth   ▷ Texture: Rough   ① ② ③ ④ ⑤ ⑥ ⑦ ⑧ ⑨

▷ Dimension: 3D   ▷ Flat   ① ② ③ ④ ⑤ ⑥ ⑦ ⑧ ⑨

When you evaluate and recognize the form and intensity of a cognitive event's sub-modalities, in NLP we call it "eliciting the sub-modalities". You might be tempted to skip ahead and begin "scratching" the visual mental movies in an attempt to eliminate bad memories. In fact, we strongly advise against it.Negative memories can be difficult to deal with, and it's understandable that many people would prefer to forget them. However, there are several reasons why this may not be a good idea, and why it may be more beneficial to simply dampen the emotional response to negative memories rather than attempting to eliminate them entirely.

To begin with, negative memories serve an important purpose in our lives. They assist us in learning from our mistakes and avoiding them in the future. For example, if we have a negative memory of being burned by a hot stove, we will be more cautious in the future. If we remove this negative memory, we may be more likely to make the same mistake and get burned again.

Furthermore, negative memories can assist us in developing empathy and understanding for others. By recalling a negative experience, we can gain insight into how others are feeling and offer support and comfort.

Another reason we don't want to get rid of bad memories is that they are a part of our personal history and identity. They contribute to who we are and how we perceive the world. While it may be appealing to try to erase negative memories and only focus on the positive, doing so may result in a distorted view of ourselves and our experiences. Finally, it is critical to acknowledge that erasing negative memories is not always possible, and that attempting to do so can be emotionally draining. It is normal to have negative memories, and it is important to learn to cope with them rather than suppress or erase them. So, what is the point of using visual sub-modalities shifting on memories? How can changes of sub-modalities help you cope better with negative memories?

This type of sub-modality work is not intended to erase or suppress the memory itself, but rather to help you gain distance and perspective from it so that the automatic recall of impressive mental movies and the accompanying thoughts no longer bother you as much. As you gain experience, you may find that you are better able to control the feelings brought on by the memory, freeing you to concentrate on what is happening right now, or what we call "current reality." As opposed to being a helpless bystander, you can actively shape your future by retaining the valuable information (content) you've recognized from your past recollections while significantly reducing the adverse effects of such memories.

Now have some fun and experiment. See how your feelings shift as you increase or decrease the intensity of your visual sub-modalities. For example, in the sub-modality Motion - f it's a motionless photograph, turn it into a movie. If it's a movie, choose a snapshot from it that can represent the whole event. Just remember to put the attributes back to normal afterwards so you don't ruin the joy you experience by thinking about the event).

Motion:

Perceptual Position (associated / dissociated):

Color/Black & White:

Size:

Dimension (2D / 3D):

Spatial location (Left / Right / Up / Down):

Proportions:

Brightness:

Contrast (Vibrant / Damp):

Distance (How far from your face):

Texture (Smooth / Rough):

Focus (In Focus / Blurred / Semi-blurred):

Visual Data (Specific exaggerated details):

Global shape:

Frame:

Overall external movement (Solid / Wobble):

Speed of thought:

Orientation:

Perspective:

Variety:

Insights: what did you learn about yourself from this exercise?

Memory (title):

Visual Sub-modalities Elicitation   Intensity

▷ Movie   ▷ Still Image   ① ② ③ ④ ⑤ ⑥ ⑦ ⑧ ⑨

▷ Associated   ▷ Dissociated   ① ② ③ ④ ⑤ ⑥ ⑦ ⑧ ⑨

▷ Color   ▷ Black & White   ① ② ③ ④ ⑤ ⑥ ⑦ ⑧ ⑨

▷ Location: ↑ → ↓ ←   ① ② ③ ④ ⑤ ⑥ ⑦ ⑧ ⑨

▷ Distance: Close ▷ Distance: Far   ① ② ③ ④ ⑤ ⑥ ⑦ ⑧ ⑨

▷ Light: Dim   ▷ Light: Bright   ① ② ③ ④ ⑤ ⑥ ⑦ ⑧ ⑨

▷ Contrast: Vibrant ▷ Contrast: Damp   ① ② ③ ④ ⑤ ⑥ ⑦ ⑧ ⑨

▷ Size: Small   ▷ Size: Large   ① ② ③ ④ ⑤ ⑥ ⑦ ⑧ ⑨

▷ Focus: Sharp   ▷ Focus: Blurr   ① ② ③ ④ ⑤ ⑥ ⑦ ⑧ ⑨

▷ Speed: Slow   ▷ Speed: Fast   ① ② ③ ④ ⑤ ⑥ ⑦ ⑧ ⑨

▷ Panoramic   ▷ Framed   ① ② ③ ④ ⑤ ⑥ ⑦ ⑧ ⑨

▷ Texture: Smooth ▷ Texture: Rough   ① ② ③ ④ ⑤ ⑥ ⑦ ⑧ ⑨

▷ Dimension: 3D   ▷ Flat   ① ② ③ ④ ⑤ ⑥ ⑦ ⑧ ⑨

Here is a new daily script for you to use over the next 30 days. The instructions are the same as for the first script in the book. Keep a log of your early morning dreams and insights (in the form on the next page). You might experience some anxiety as a result of this particular script, especially given the ambiguous nature of the magician's character. Make notes as these sensations and images occur to you so that you can process them later. These are indicators of the hidden regions of your mental maps.

Day	Date	Insights / Early Morning Dreams
1		
2		
3		
4		
5		
6		
7		
8		
9		
10		

Day	Date	Insights / Early Morning Dreams
11		
12		
13		
14		
15		
16		
17		
18		
19		
20		

Day	Date	Insights / Early Morning Dreams
21		
22		
23		
24		
25		
26		
27		
28		
29		
30		

"Please Don't Judge Me!"

The spotlight effect is the tendency to overestimate how much attention others pay to us and our motives. When we are unsure of ourselves or how others see us, we may worry that others are passing judgment on us or rejecting us. This can lead to feelings of restlessness and insecurity, which in turn can increase anxiety about being rejected.

You know you're in trouble when you experience hesitance and anxiety whenever you're compelled to interact with another person outside of your closest social circle, and you desperately hope that this person will not criticize or judge you in any way. A groveling, almost-crying voice within you may beg, "Please don't judge me! Please don't judge me! Pleeeeeeeeeeease don't judge me!" and you get to feel a sense of relief when the interaction is over without you getting rejected in some way or, even better, if the person is giving you a genuine compliment.

The nausea brought on by unwarranted anxiety is only one of the problems with this orientation. In reality, the situation is far more intricate. Having such a purposeless, subjective experience has devastating effects on your chances of growth and progress. First, you immediately become needy and a people-pleaser, saying or doing anything to reduce the possibility of that person rejecting you. This means you'll come across as unauthentic and somewhat manipulative to them.

Second, your mind will continually try to protect you from having such subjective experiences again because of the emotional toll they take. To what extent does this apply? You'll miss out on discovering new people, expanding your professional network, making more sales calls, asking for a pay raise, striking up a conversation with someone you find attractive, and countless other opportunities. What do we call this type of avoidance behavior? That's right, it's the dreaded fear of being rejected. By thinking, "Please don't judge me!" you are allowing yourself to be trapped in this cycle.

However, there is a third consequence, and it is probably this psychological impact that led you to pick up this book in the first place. When your mind represents a desired outcome, especially something you desperately want, a part of you replays the potential rejection scenario in full detail in a corresponding and larger-than-life colorful and impressive mental movie. It is your ego's feeble attempt to predict the unknowable future and keep you safe at all costs, including at the expense of your sense of satisfaction with life itself.

Then you go out into the world and are forced to interact with "unsafe" people, and because of your own subjective experiences of rejection, you view these people as larger than life and intimidating, making you feel small and inferior. That's how your rejection anxiety gets activated and induced at the worst possible times. The moment you get the chance to make a positive change, try something new, or even just fall in love with someone who likes you back, your ego steps in and sabotages your efforts. Your chances of succeeding through pure chance are extremely low unless the other person is exceptionally intriguing and can squeeze through your defenses; furthermore, they must be more proactive and desire the exact same thing as you do.

Keep in mind the formula we discussed earlier:

The event is a given: you are talking to someone you don't know well enough and who is outside your innermost social circle.

The reaction—the behavioral choice you make—is a cautious one. There's a good reason for this: Your older self had a really harrowing experience with random people who were out to push you down and humiliate you into submission. The implicit, often inaudible message from your unconsciousness is that this person is not "safe" because they may not be / are not concerned with or interested in your well-being.

Your closest friends and family members (hopefully) are "safe" because they have repeatedly shown an interest in taking care of you and helping you out. They have shown appreciation for who you are, not just what you do for them. Anyone outside of that small circle may cause you emotional harm, so they are labeled "unsafe" or "dangerous" until proven otherwise.

Rejection anxiety is a physiological and psychological response to the combination of a factual event (talking to someone) and a choice of behavior (caution, alarm bells firing, hesitation, inauthentic communication, etc.). We began this book by listing a variety of symptoms, and you have already chosen your own set of repeated subjective experiences. Later, you investigated the behavioral choices that resulted in these unfortunate negative subjective experiences, and you devised alternative choices that could have resulted in different, more interesting, and positive subjective experiences.

So how do you snap out of the "Please don't judge me!" attitude?

Consider the implications of this attitude: What is the inherent presupposition in pleading that someone not judge you? that this person has the authority to make a decision about you. The concept of judgment is expanding beyond the binary of reward and punishment. Someone's "judging" you harshly if you interpret their averted gaze or disapproving expression as a personal criticism of who you are. Again, we've said it before and will say it again: external events have no direct effect on your emotions. In current reality, your emotions are the results of your behavioral choices.

This is an important point, so read it again and again until it becomes ingrained in your mind. Because this person appears larger than you do in your mental representation of the world, you give that fictional image more authority over how you feel about yourself. You perceive them in a standard fashion, but in your mind's eye, their "persona" is larger and more dramatic than it actually is. You have learned in previous chapters that you do not directly interact with reality but rather with mental representations of it. So your pleading, "Please don't judge me," is a reaction to how you interpret that moment of meeting that person, rather than to the event itself. It's not the person who made you feel this way; it's how you have represented him or her in your mind, in real time, while they're speaking to you.

Keeping in mind what you know about the visual representational system at this point, what do you think you can do to mitigate the effects of this mindset the next time you meet someone who is more accomplished than you, more attractive than you, or even an actual authority figure, and you find yourself feeling intimidated or inferior?

Ideally, the solution sprang immediately to mind: you quickly elicit the most influential (or "driving") sub-modality and reduce it back to its normal setting, based on reality. If the person's visual representation appears to be too large, you reduce it to his or her normal size. You can make the colors fade and dull if they're too bright and vivid. To avoid getting lost in your own thoughts while someone else is talking to you, you don't need to go through the entire list of sub-modalities. There's no reason this process should take more than 1 or 2 seconds at most. You become aware of the feeling, and you immediately examine your mental image to identify what stands out and is exaggerated. If the size is an issue, you reduce it.If it's a location, you return it to its proper place, and so on.

Over-modifying the mental image is something you definitely do not want to end up doing. It's tempting to make that mental image of the other person so tiny that you dwarf them. You can imagine the problems that could arise: You might automatically make behavioral choices that project arrogance or aggression, and if that is inappropriate in that situation, you'll be in big trouble.

The "normal" function is emphasized because of this. You normalize the exaggerated sub-modalities in accordance with the current reality. If that person is 6 feet 5 inches tall and the top of your head is at his chest level, you shrink the mental image to that size. It needs to be

113

grounded in factual evidence, not your inflated sense of self-importance. Use caution, and especially while mid-conversation, avoid making too many abrupt changes. You should stick to the sub-modality you have identified as dominant, switch it up quickly, and then jump back into the conversation.

If you feel anxious about meeting someone new later in the week, you can set aside some time to work on it and go through the visual representational system's sub-modalities more slowly and deliberately; the same rule applies: reduce the sub-modalities to their correct visual dimensions and characteristics in accordance with current reality. Practice this several times at different intervals in the days leading up to the meeting, and notice how your behavioral choices in real time differ, as do the emotions you feel in your subjective experience.

Unfazed by Your Inner Critic

Is the old adage that "sticks and stones may break my bones, but words will never break me" just a bunch of hooey, or is it possible to protect oneself from the psychological and emotional damage that can result from having to experience verbal abuse? Of course it's possible. People like our old friend Lucky Joe do this all the time. They appear to be completely immune to unfair criticism or gossip directed at them. They shrug it off as if it were complete nonsense. How exactly do they do that, and how can you learn to do the same?

Verbal harassment can come from either an external or internal source. The first category is what we refer to as "outsourcing," because it is provided by a third party and is often classified as a favor. To them, it's in your best interest to be criticized so that you can grow from the experience, own up to your shortcomings, and adjust your behavior to meet their standards. We "outsource" when we allow the other person to verbally abuse us and actually listen, despite the fact that we know it's unfair criticism. When we take in and internalize verbal abuse instead of rejecting it, we "outsource" our free will and rights.

The second kind is entirely self-inflicted. Listen to your thoughts. You can actually hear a voice inside your head. Most people's inner auditory experience is that of a voice emanating from their own vocal chords, even though no outward sound is actually being produced. Some people may even move their lips or jaw muscles as they speak word by word to themselves, as if muted or lip-syncing. That chatter in your mind is usually a collection of different parts of your personality arguing over the meaning of your thoughts.

Stop reading for a moment and tune in to your inner monologue. What is your mind telling you right now?

When that voice is critical, judgmental, and full of self-loathing, it's generated by an ego defense mechanism. No one has actually spoken to you, but it feels as though there's a voice projected very close to you, perpetually belittling and berating you. How can your own self-induced internal voice offend its owner? "Why was I so dumb?", "I'm ugly; of course she wouldn't like me,", "I'm a loser," and so on.

An internal voice can be associated or disassociated. Whenever you find yourself saying, "I can't believe I just did that!" or "I got this!" that is an associated experience. You use the first person singular, in the realm of "I am."

Dissociated inner voice examples:

"I can do this!"

"I wish I knew this back then"

"I feel lonely, I don't have many friends"

"Now how do I get from here to there? Hmmm…"

When you talk to yourself as if you were someone else, like when you say things like, "How can you be so stupid?!" or "Look at what you've done! What a moron!" It is a dissociated experience. Who is criticizing whom, exactly? It's as if you're playing a mental role inside your head that has the power to evaluate your entire person. This is probably the most common method of harsh self-criticism, but it is also logically flawed. Is there a court where the accused could act as the prosecutor? You take on such a persona not for the sake of personal development or learning from your errors, but rather to relive past emotional states, even if they are unpleasant, because these are sensations you already know and understand, making them less risky than creating something new.

Dissociated inner voice examples:

"Nobody likes you, so why are you surprised?"

"Of course she wouldn't notice you, look at you, you're so ugly"

"You have no chance; you really want to fail? Again?!"

"You're going to make a fool of yourself. Go ahead! All you get in this life is humiliation…"

"That guy looks much smarter than you are, so expect to fail"

Our minds operate largely on autopilot. We think by way of mental movies and internal monologues. Our thoughts are either visualized or heard. On a daily basis, the human mind generates around 50,000 thoughts. Most of the time, we have little control over what we allow into our minds. Thoughts appear seemingly from nowhere. You can't force yourself to only think the thoughts you would like to think. As with the external world, it is impossible to exert total conscious dominion over one's own body and mind. If your blood sugar drops, your mind might interpret that as despair and start looking for explanations for why you're feeling down. That will make you think about things that have made you unhappy in the past or things that could make you unhappy in the future. Fear of rejection is stimulated, at least to an extent, by unfairly criticizing yourself.

Thoughts are notoriously fast, and move rapidly, but they always appear in current reality. They are an integral part of your experience right here and now. And because thoughts are generated by, and experienced by, your mind alone - you have the cognitive choice to translate them in whatever manner you'd like.

Record some of your more hurtful and less productive self-talk from the last few weeks:

These words you heard in your head are not digital and flat; they have nuance, depth, and meaning. Your internal monologue has characteristics—features that are emphasized in order to grab your attention and make you feel things kinesthetically in your body. These characteristics are the auditory representational system's sub-modalities.

Maintain the same content when working on changing the sub-modalities of your self-talk, no matter how morbid and hateful the words are. "You are the worst person alive; you should be dead!" Or "look at you, you're disgusting!", "Who would ever want to be with someone so hideous?", "Stupid! Stupid! Stupid!", "you always screw it up, don't you?", And so on. Even so: don't change a word; leave the sentences as they are.

The next step is to deliberately relive the internal voice while attempting a new interpretation. Consider this scenario: As you ride the bus, someone turns to you and unleashes a barrage of insults and curses, specifically designed for you and how you look like. How would you respond? What if he says, "I'm so sorry, I have Tourette syndrome, and I can't control it," right after? What response would you have in that situation? Isn't it true that although the words are the same, the interpretation (your individual and subjective perception of it) is not? So, who says you can't take the same approach with each and every biased and unfair voice?

Another thing to consider is that you tend to pick up on (and translate internally) what you expect to hear. The vast majority of us are guilty of selective hearing. In most cases, our minds are constantly filling in the gaps in our comprehension of what was actually said. Therefore, what we eventually claim to have heard is typically a combination of the original words spoken and the gaps our psyches fill in. Our minds' additions to spoken words are frequently accentuated auditory sub-modalities. And the meaning of any digital format depends on its qualities or attributes, not its content, just as we have seen with the visual representational system.

Review the instances of destructive internal dialogue that you just listed.

If you want (which means you make a behavioral choice) to feel bad about yourself, imagine your inner voice talking to you in a mean way. Increase the volume and bring it closer to your face. Incorporate a deep, "heavy," bassy tonality. Construct a stereo rendition. Highlight the most offensive words. That's a big part of what you've done so far, and it's what has probably made you nervous about the potential of being rejected.

Let's do something entertaining now. Imagine one of the phrases you wrote down being said to you in the most alluring and enticing voice you can think of. Think of the seductive whispers of Marlyn Monroe, Barry White, or any other highly sensual voice. It's interesting how the same words can sound completely different when someone is trying to seduce you. In light of the fact that this is a book and we can't exactly "talk" to you, let us demonstrate with some pictures instead. Of course, do not imagine a person in your mind; just hear the voice; do not use the visual representational system, only the auditory one.

How do you feel when you imagine the same harsh words spoken in a seductive and welcoming voice?

Is there a noticeable difference between this and your previous interpretation of the same words? Kinesthetically speaking (through your body's sensations), how does it feel different? Can you pinpoint exactly where you're experiencing this change? Does the new meaning bring any sighs of relief or even excitement?

Now choose a different phrase from your list of negative self-talk. This time, imagine the voice to have a very high pitch (perhaps the vocal qualities of Mickey Mouse) and to be approximately 10 feet in front of you. How does it make you feel?

Does this interpretation differ significantly from how you previously interpreted the same words? How does it feel different kinesthetically (through your physical sensations)? Can you point out exactly where this change is happening? Are there any sighs of relief or even laughter at the new meaning?

Auditory Sub-modalities Elicitation — Intensity

▷ Self-Talk: Own Voice   ▷ Self-Talk: Other Voice   ① ② ③ ④ ⑤ ⑥ ⑦ ⑧ ⑨

▷ Pitch: Low   ▷ Pitch: High   ① ② ③ ④ ⑤ ⑥ ⑦ ⑧ ⑨

▷ Content   ▷ Syntax / Form   ① ② ③ ④ ⑤ ⑥ ⑦ ⑧ ⑨

▷ Emotional Expression   ① ② ③ ④ ⑤ ⑥ ⑦ ⑧ ⑨

▷ Volume: Low   ▷ Volume: High   ① ② ③ ④ ⑤ ⑥ ⑦ ⑧ ⑨

▷ Harmonic   ▷ Disharmonic   ① ② ③ ④ ⑤ ⑥ ⑦ ⑧ ⑨

▷ Tempo: Fast   ▷ Tempo: Slow   ① ② ③ ④ ⑤ ⑥ ⑦ ⑧ ⑨

▷ Location In Space: ① ② ③ ④ ⑤ ⑥ ⑦ ⑧ ⑨

▷ Monotonic   ▷ Inflections   ① ② ③ ④ ⑤ ⑥ ⑦ ⑧ ⑨

▷ Long Speech   ▷ Short Bursts   ① ② ③ ④ ⑤ ⑥ ⑦ ⑧ ⑨

▷ Key Words (digital):   ① ② ③ ④ ⑤ ⑥ ⑦ ⑧ ⑨

Here are the main sub-modalities of the auditory representational system:

Self-talk / Foreign:

Is the voice you hear your own or someone else's? Do you recognize the source of that voice? Is it a part of you (a personality trait) that takes a stand and makes an argument, or is it repetitive rambling you've heard before?

Volume:

How loud is it? Does it stay at the same volume throughout, or does it go up and down in volume?

Thickness:

How thick or "heavy" the voice is, or how smooth and "cushy"? Voices with more weight and thickness come across as more authoritative and serious than those with less.

Tempo:

How fast or how slow is the speech? Does it alternate between fast forwarding and slowing down?

Location:

Do you hear it from within or from without? Is it as if you're creating the voice with your own vocal cords (outwards), or as if someone is speaking to you from within your mind (inwards)? If you could place your hand on the source of the voice, where would it be located in your spatial surroundings?

Surround:

In relation to location, do you hear the voice in mono or stereo? Is there a sense of reverb or echo to the voice, and do the inflections seem to emanate from all directions (surround)?

Pitch:

Is the pitch high or low? How high and how low? Is the internal voice based on a real voice (yours or others')? Does the voice's pitch sound higher than in reality (normal), lower, or just about the same?

Melody:

Does the voice sound monotonous, or does it sound more melodic with changes in tones (like musical phrases)?

Tonality:

Which end of the tonal spectrum does it fall on—nasal, vibrant, thin, jarring?

Rhythm:

Is there enough rhythm in the speech that it sounds like a beat, maybe even one that could be accompanied with drums?

Inflection:

When you listen carefully, what sounds or phrases do you notice being emphasized?

Continuity:

Does the voice stutter or pauses intermittently? Or is it continuous and fluid?

Pay close attention to the location sub-modality. It turns out that shifting the location of a voice is a simple method to modify its effect.

Think back and consider a voice in your head that was making you feel uneasy, recall that internal experience and note where it is in relation to your body. The majority of the time, the voices you hear will appear to be coming from inside your skull or very close to it, as if someone is whispering in your ears. Where does it come from? Is it from inside your head or somewhere else? The question is whether it is in front, behind, to the left, to the right, or elsewhere.

Consider its orientation: is it pointed at you or away from you?

Point in the direction the sound is traveling and indicate where it is coming from. When you hear a voice outside of your head, it almost always points directly at you. You can also use an arrow to draw its path.

Change the direction the voice is pointing and notice how your perception of it changes. This is something that most people have never considered. Allow that voice to change course. This usually indicates that it is now pointing away from your face. How does it change how you feel about its message?

Then, try listening to the voice when it's pointing toward and away from you to compare the two. In this circumstance, certain statements may seem as though they are directed towards you, while others may sound as though they are directed away from you and fading away. How does it make you feel, and what is the main difference between the two orientations?

Consider whether there is a difference when it points straight up and straight down, or when it points left or right, forward or backward. If there is, what is it and in which direction is it more prominent?

The volume of the voice and your reaction time are both reduced when it is directed away from you. Most people find it easier and more acceptable to listen to what a disturbing voice is saying when it is pointing away from them.

When it's in the middle of those two directions, you're more inclined to react emotionally, as you feel you're in the center or at the apex of that dramatic voice. That's usually the format in which self-blame, guilt, and shame are manufactured internally in the auditory representational system.

The next step is to experiment with varying the voice's location to observe how hearing the same voice from different places in space impacts your emotional responses and overall impressions.

To begin with, focus on the sensation you get as you listen to the voice coming from your left hip. How does it make you feel?

Your critical voice is less forceful when it originates from your hip. When you do this, alter the tone of the voice as well. You may notice a gradual decrease in intensity and rhythm as well as in your own emotional responses.

Take note of how you feel when you hear this voice from your tail bone:

Examine how it feels when the same voice emanates from your right ankle:

Pay attention to what happens when you listen to the voice if it comes from your heart's center and the depths of your soul (if you immediately imagined an exorcism, that's about right):

Next, listen to the voice coming from your left index finger and pay attention to how it feels:

Experiment with how it feels to hear that voice coming from somewhere else on your body. Play around with different locations, and take note of how it makes you feel in each one:

Finally, put that voice back in its original position and with its original tonality. Now that you've gone through plenty of experiments, recall the voice in its original format and consider how much your reaction to the voice in its original place has changed:

If you must hear a terrible voice, it's usually preferable to do so from a great distance rather than from within your own skull, and certainly not from within the depth of your soul. Hearing a voice in your chest is unsettling, and the accompanying emotion is sometimes misunderstood as anxiety, despair, or agony. It can be distressing and difficult to make sense of one's own inner voice if that voice isn't particularly pleasant or clear. Even though it is harmful and can lead to severe emotional storms, many people do this habitually without even realizing it is their own behavioral choice, and they can control it any moment they choose to, just as you have experienced it now.

Now test your newfound skill. Review what you've learned so far about your critical inner voice and ask yourself, "From which location did I generally feel safe hearing this distressing voice?" Recall the same voice and allow it to come from that location. How do you feel about it now?

129

You already have an intuitive understanding of the following reasoning: people who value your identity, time, and efforts will want to support you and enable you to feel more at ease around them. Those who are jealous or poorly mannered will try to do the opposite. Identifying friends and foes in this manner is a great strategy. It has been said that true friends are those who know everything there is to know about you and still love you. You may want to limit your interactions with those who, despite knowing little about you, act superior in their judgments. They aren't. That's why they're so quick to pass judgment on other people: their own insecurities are causing them to act out in destructive ways.

Lastly, the ultimate question you ought to be able to answer by now is: would you ever have the audacity to talk to someone else uttering the same nasty messages your critical voice is telling you? And if you would not dare to do so, risking getting beat up brutally, why on earth would you allow your ego to violate your inner peace in the same way?

Because you cannot and should not control the words of others, your best option is to brush them off and move on, even if it's a voice inside your head. Lucky Joe knows how to do this. With the help of sub-modalities, you now know how to do this too. All you have to do is practice and have fun with it until it becomes habitual.

The following is a brand-new script for your use over the next 30 days. The instructions are the same as for the first script in this book. A tracking form for early morning dreams is also provided. Before continuing, it's essential that you use this script consistently for at least a week because it serves as a preparation for what we'll do next. During that time, you ought to go back over your written responses, revise the parts you think are less genuine or truthful, and add any new detail your mind has come up with.

Close your eyes and take a few deep breaths, allowing yourself to fully relax and let go of any tension in your body. As you exhale, imagine yourself releasing all of the stress and negativity that has been weighing you down.

Imagine yourself standing in a dark, damp cave. You feel the rough, cold walls against your skin and the musty smell of the cave fills your nostrils. You see that you are confined in massive chains that are anchored to the walls of the cave.

The chains are made of thick, rusted metal, and they feel heavy and constricting on your body. You can see the deep grooves and scars on the chains, evidence of past attempts to break free.

The chains represent the limiting beliefs that are holding you back and preventing you from reaching your full potential. These beliefs may be thoughts like "I'm not good enough," "I can't do it," or "I'm not worthy of success." You feel weighed down and trapped by these beliefs.

But as you stand there, you decide that you are ready to break free. You take a deep breath and focus your attention on the chains that are holding you back.

Slowly, you begin to intentionally erode the chains with steady, consistent effort. You visualize yourself chipping away at the links of the chain with a small hammer, one by one, until they become weaker and weaker. As you work on the chains, you may feel a sense of resistance or discomfort, as these limiting beliefs are deeply ingrained and may be difficult to let go of.

You focus your energy and attention on breaking free from these chains, imagining yourself swinging the hammer with determination and purpose. You visualize the sparks flying off of the chains as you make progress, slowly but surely.

As you continue to chip away at the chains, you start to feel a sense of hope and determination rising within you. You know that it will take time and effort to break free, but you are determined to do it. You visualize yourself becoming stronger and more resilient as you work on the chains, building up the muscles in your arms and chest.

After what feels like an eternity, you finally break free from the chains that were holding you back. You feel a sense of elation and freedom as you step out of the cave and into the sunlight. You are no longer confined by your limiting beliefs, and you are free to pursue your dreams and reach your full potential.

As you stand in the sunlight, take a moment to bask in the feeling of freedom and possibility. Imagine all of the things that you are now capable of achieving now that you are no longer held back by your limiting beliefs. Allow yourself to feel proud and confident in your ability to overcome any obstacle that comes your way.

Take a few more deep breaths and when you're ready, slowly open your eyes. Remember that you have the power to break free from limiting beliefs and reach your full potential. Just be patient and consistent in your efforts, and you will eventually succeed. Allow yourself to carry this feeling of confidence and determination with you throughout your day.

Day	Date	Insights / Early Morning Dreams
1		
2		
3		
4		
5		
6		
7		
8		
9		
10		

Day	Date	Insights / Early Morning Dreams
11		
12		
13		
14		
15		
16		
17		
18		
19		
20		

Day	Date	Insights / Early Morning Dreams
21		
22		
23		
24		
25		
26		
27		
28		
29		
30		

From Fear to Freedom - Breaking the Chains

Mindful attention to repetitive thoughts may reveal hidden motivations and conflicts (what we call in NLP the "deep structure"). Here are some examples of common repetitive thoughts disguised as improvement-oriented questions:

"How can I be so stupid?"

"Why can't I seem to get anything right?"

"Why am I so weak?"

"Why do I always make such a mess of things?"

"Why can't I get anything right? Why am so useless?"

"Why do I deserve to be such a failure?"

"Why am I so awkward and cringy?"

"Why am I so ugly? Why nobody likes me?"

"Why do I keep making the same idiotic mistakes?"

"Why do I always let people step all over me?"

Core beliefs are not easily found and recognized. Our core beliefs are our most fundamental and deeply held convictions about ourselves, other people, and the world. These convictions shape our attitudes, behaviors, and actions and influence how we take in, make sense of, and respond to the world around us. Because they occur on autopilot, we may be blissfully ignorant of the ways in which they shape our actions and perceptions. Core beliefs can be positive or negative and may be based on a variety of factors, including our upbringing, culture, personal experiences, and exposure to different ideas and perspectives. They may also be influenced by our emotional states and can be reinforced through repetitive thoughts and behaviors. For example, someone who has a core belief that they are not capable or worthy may tend to shy away from new challenges and opportunities, develop fear of rejection or fear of failure, while someone who has a core belief that they are capable and worthy may be more likely to pursue their goals and aspirations.

The current climate in the West perpetuates rejection anxiety by promoting the "hustle" mentality: if you fail to succeed, it is your own fault because you haven't worked hard enough. Since the results you achieve are directly proportional to your level of effort, you have every reason to feel embarrassed and guilty. While this problematic belief has spread like wildfire, it is incorrect on so many levels that it frequently leads people to seek shortcuts, fall victim to scams, and develop psychological issues. It's just another version of a rat race, except you're chained and compelled to pretend they're not there.

A second fallacy is the belief that one can duplicate another person's success simply by adopting their habits and attempting to make the same choices in life. Unfortunately, gurus who claimed to have scientific proof for their techniques and used NLP as the basis for their marketing made that false assumption widely accepted. Using the same strategies as someone else may produce similar outcomes, but these gains would be internal rather than external. When discussing strategies in the context of NLP, we only ever talk about mental maneuvers. Copying Jeff Bezos's or Warren Buffett's wardrobe choices won't make you as wealthy as they are. Their successes are influenced by far too many factors that are outside of their or your control. This in no way precludes the desire for extreme wealth, if that is what your heart desires. This really means that you don't dismiss the importance of seizing opportunities in the right place at the right time, although you cannot predict it, market needs and conditions, other people's decisions, luck, and other factors in determining whether or not you strike gold. If you've wondered why there seems to have been a surge in the number of self-help gurus and success coaches in recent years, it's because many people, sooner or later, came to realize that selling the fantasy to others is a more efficacious way to generate revenue. It's perfectly fine to aim as high as you want, but for all the right reasons, including your mental health, keep your feet on the ground. Maintain your connection to current reality and respond to what is happening rather than what you have learned to fear or what your ego tells you to wish for.

Your personal and professional goals will benefit greatly from your decreased habitual fear of rejection. It will not, however, guarantee riches or the adoration of others. What it really means is that you aren't letting your inner conflicts dampen your enthusiasm and willingness to experiment and experience what could be when you come across suitable and appropriate opportunities, regardless of whether or not you end up winning that opportunity. In the simplest terms, if you don't even try, you're guaranteed to fail. What we've done so far in the book is re-establish your command over the mental routines that have been clouding your judgment in the present moment. We're going to delve much deeper from here until the end of the book. Keep in mind that while emotional pain may emerge as a result, if you (choose to) let it be instead of trying to push it away, it will serve the same function as disinfecting an open wound. It's painful and yet necessary to prevent further complications and assist the body in self-healing.

Because of the profound effect that our fundamental beliefs can have on our daily lives, it is crucial that we examine and question these convictions more often. A more fulfilling and meaningful life can be achieved by identifying and challenging negative core beliefs and cultivating positive ones.

It's painful and yet necessary to prevent further complications and assist the body in self-healing. It's easy to identify the self-limiting beliefs you hold when you listen to your critical inner voice. However, there are underlying core beliefs that you have yet to reveal. The exercise below will assist you in exposing some of them. Before proceeding, ensure that you are well rested and that you feel strong and capable of handling emotional turmoil today.

Just breathe deeply for a moment before you respond to each question. Repeat the question aloud, and jot down the answer that comes to mind immediately.

What do I often worry about or feel anxious about?

What do I often feel frustrated about in myself?

What do I often feel frustrated about in others? (Think beyond words and actions; consider everything you can perceive about them with your senses: body posture, attitude or approach to life, how they handle time or problems, how they dress or carry themselves, and so on.)

What do I often feel like I'm not good enough at/for or not capable of doing?

Don't just write "love" or "money, investigate further and describe actual subjective experiences you feel you are not lucky enough to experience, such as "getting a warm hug from someone who loves me unconditionally" or "getting an A+ in the final exam." Instead of simply writing "love" or "money," go deeper and describe specific, subjective experiences you feel you've never had (or will never have again), such as "getting a warm hug from someone who loves me unconditionally" or "getting an A+ on the final exam."

What do I often feel that I'm not worthy of or deserving of?

What do I often feel like I'm not able (ever) to achieve or accomplish?

What do I often feel I'm not good enough for or not good enough to have or own?

What do I often feel that I'm not able to change or improve in myself, no matter how painful it is or how hard I try?

What do I often feel that I'm not able to change or improve in my circumstances or environment? (Including family, relationships, workplace, etc.)

What do I often feel that I'm never going to be able to overcome or succeed in?

141

Core beliefs are lurking underground, deep inside your unconscious mind. They are not all a hindrance. Some of these core beliefs are highly essential and helpful. For example, one common positive core belief is the wordless "I can walk like the big people around me", which you had when you were a toddler. If you had the opposite, limiting, belief, we would see you crawling around in your 30's. Without the conviction you can do something, although you'e attempted it a hundred times and fell on your bums, you would not be fighting gravity to lift yourself off the ground. Hopefully, that belief was also encouraged and supported by your caregivers at the time, and it became a pleasant and self value affirming experience.

What do I often feel that I'm never going to be able to overcome or succeed in? Reflect on the questions and your answers above. Do you notice the common denominator among them? They're grounded in a small sample of objective reality and a large sample of personal interpretation (mental movies). You have a high capacity for one-trial learning, as was stated earlier in the book. That's the kind of learning that leads one to form firm convictions as a result of a single event. The feeling associated with it may be positive or negative.

Assumptions form the basis of all beliefs. These beliefs ring true because their underlying assumptions are rationalized as serving the interests of the believer. When you read it on paper, a self-limiting belief like "nobody likes me" sounds awful. But in reality, that belief is a component of your rejection anxiety, and as we've established, rejection anxiety causes you to avoid taking risks, which means you never have to feel the humiliating humiliation of being rejected. The assumptions are solid, and the belief feels right and true to reality because it is based on previous experiences, both external (actual past events) and internal (self-talk rumination and mental movies). This self-limiting belief is the invisible chain that keeps you safe within the comfort zone of the familiar. The links in that chain represent the belief's underlying assumptions. The stronger the links, the more difficult or even impossible it is to break the chain.

We can increase our chances of breaking the chain by deliberately weakening the links, as you might expect. Instead of making a grand gesture, like a gigantic gladiator smashing the shackles, we deliberately and persistently cast doubt on the assumptions that hold that belief together. As a result, the chain's integrity is undermined, and the assumptions no longer serve any purpose in the present, allowing the core limiting belief to be swapped out for a more realistic and beneficial one.

Rather than being a victim of your fear, you destabilize its authority and thus find freedom.

There are numerous tools available to help us weaken core limiting beliefs, many of which are too advanced and complicated to cover in a single book. There are numerous tools available to help us weaken core limiting beliefs, many of which are too advanced and complicated to cover in a single book. The good news is that we still have access to highly efficient methods we can put to use right away. Cartesian coordinates are one of them. Seeing a therapist may be necessary if you have difficulty altering your underlying limiting beliefs despite applying the strategies discussed here. Even if self-therapy doesn't work for you, it's still a good idea to give it a shot. The silver lining is that we can still make use of highly effective strategies. One of these is the inquiry into cartesian coordinates.

In a cause and event dynamics, there are four distinct options (C=cause, E=Event):

C → E - Theorem - What must happen if you did X?

C ⊗ E - Converse - What will not happen if you did X?

C ⊗ → E - Inverse - What will happen if you did not do X?

C ⊗ → E ⊗ - Reverse - What will not happen if you did not do X?

Notice how the last option is the negation (we call it the non-mirror reverse image) of the first. The last question is: what could not be? It is what the action you wish to take does not consist of in terms of consequences. If the theorem is irrelevant to the person, it will no longer be a problem in the non-mirror image reverse pattern. Everything that the cause does not contain is included in the non-mirror-image reverse of the issue. The issue collapses when we apply the non-mirror image reverse. This occurs as a result of a lack of causality in the non-mirror image reverse. When the assumption's validity (truthfulness) is removed, the link loses its thickness and effectiveness.

Taking into account your responses, choose one action that you wish you could take but feel you cannot due to fear of rejection, such as calling an accountant to set up an LLC for your dream business or asking that girl out on a date:

What would happen if you did?

What would not happen if you did?

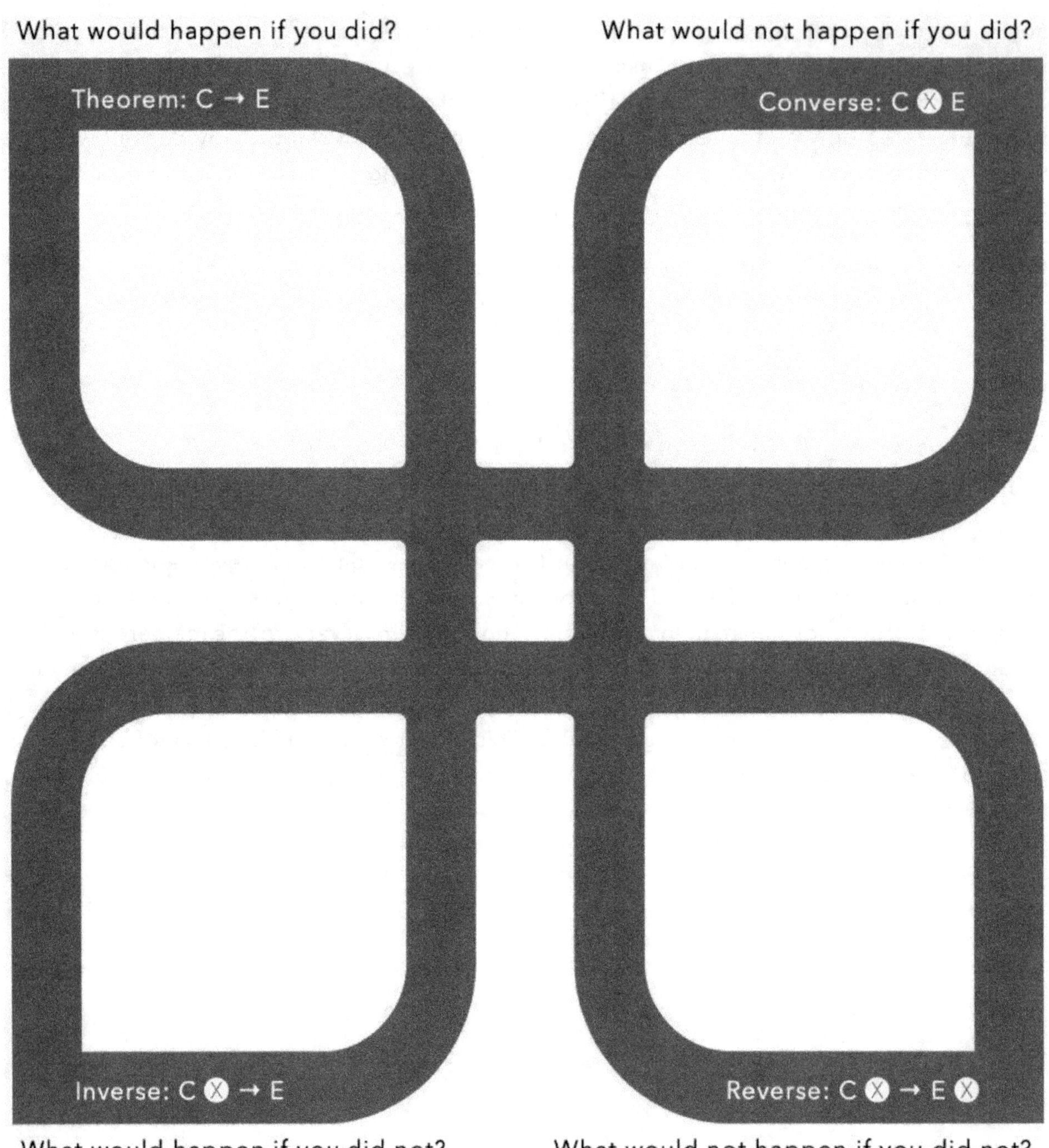

What would happen if you did not?

What would not happen if you did not?

C=cause

E=Event

The use of Cartesian coordinates helps you to question the validity of the limiting belief and open up to alternate interpretations that make more sense in the context of current reality.

Example: "I would ask Mary out on a date if I wasn't so afraid of being rejected."

C → E - Theorem - What must happen if you did ask Mary out on a date?

- *"I would feel nervous and excited and wish she would say yes"*

- *"I would definitely and undoubtedly discover finally if she likes me too, even a little"*

- *"She will be surprised because we were good friends for so long"*

- *"I will no longer need to fantasize about my chances with Mary"*

Mary will be caught off guard, you will definitely experience some anxiety or anticipation, and her response will definitely reveal whether or not you have a chance to become her boyfriend. Despite what your fear of rejection is telling you, it is not a "must" that she will find you ugly and repulsive and humiliate you in front of everyone. It is not a "must" that she humiliate you in public. She could respond by saying, "Yes! Finally!" And jump into your arms; it's still not a must. It's important to note that the question contains the word "must," which means you cannot assume or predict what someone else will do.

The reason for this is that if you are certain she will say "no" or reject you harshly, your fear of rejection has no validity in this situation and is not a limiting belief that prevents you from asking Mary out. It must be based on real evidence that she is not romantically interested in you, and you must accept this as reality. However, if your assumption is based on your "gut feeling" or anything other than a clear statement from Mary that you are not a romantic interest for her, you are deceiving yourself. Therefore, it is imperative that the "must" in the answers to this question be grounded in reality.

C ⊗ E - Converse - What will not happen if you did X?

- *"I might feel like I'm dying, but I will not actually die"*

- *"I will not lose an arm or a leg or suffer any injury"*

C ⊗ → E - Inverse - What will happen if you did not do X?

- *"I will continue to see how Mary go out with someone else and feel horrible about myself"*

- *"I will continue fantasizing and eating myself on the inside for being a lazy coward"*

C Ⓧ → E Ⓧ - Reverse - What will not happen if you did not do X?

- *"I will never know how Mary really feels about me; always guessing..."*

- *"I will certainly not be Mary's boyfriend anytime soon"*

This method of analysis has consequences. Assuming the young man in the preceding example is thinking along similar lines, he may begin to consider:

- *"If I don't ask her out now, what if she tells me when we're 50 that she was secretly hoping I would? I could miss our best years together..."*

- *"What if her next boyfriend is violent toward her? She deserves much better than this. "*

- *"The way she should be treated is how I would treat her - wish so much love and respect she'd be happy and fulfilled."*

- *"She always smiles when she sees me; I know she likes me, so let's say this coming Valentine, I'll tell her how I feel, and who knows?"*

- *"I have to be there for her and give her a chance to see me as a potential suitor."*

Working with limiting beliefs in this manner causes your unconscious mind to begin dissolving the links of the chains behind the scenes as more and more evidence is poured into it that these assumptions are false and may be a hindrance to your survival. As a result, you'll feel less threatened and have less need to engage in avoidance behaviors whenever you're confronted with situations that used to make you anxious about being rejected.

At the end of this book you'll find more copies of the cartesian coordinates form.

"I Don't Stand a Chance, So Why Bother?!"

Beliefs are necessary devices for our minds because they make navigating the world outside our bodies easier, faster, and safer. If you believe you won't be flying by flapping your arms, there's not much chance you'd be willing to walk on a wire 20 stories above the ground with no safety net below. Even though the expectation you have created for yourself is negative (the expectation that you are unable to do something), it is a very helpful belief to have if you care about your life and your body. However, the same kind of belief can limit your potential by keeping you from taking calculated risks, like pursuing an attractive person for a date, approaching your boss about a raise, or cold calling a new potential client.

Insecurities, self-doubt, and fear can cause a person to automatically view their own desires with a sense of impending disappointment. When considering taking action toward that desired outcome, their attitude (a behavioral choice) is binary: either 0 or 1. Only success or failure in reaching their objectives and fulfilling their desire exist in that person's mind. Because, really, what else could there be?

You either get the trophy or you don't; there's no middle ground in the cognitive structural dynamics of that scenario. They've won if they've gotten everything they wanted, and they've lost if they've gotten nothing or less than they wanted. Either Mary responds enthusiastically with a "yes!" or by saying "no," it is a judgment on herself as undesirable. Cartesian coordinates can initially aid in distinguishing between fantasy-based and realistic-based negative expectations. When differentiating between what is possible and what is not, however, does not alleviate fears of rejection, it is necessary to dig deeper into the nature of the individual's realistic expectations.

Do you really only have two options if you decide to take action and ask Mary out on a date? Should you limit your expectations to either hope or despair? Is it truly all or nothing, with the outcome being either euphoria or the most painful failure imaginable?

When you decide to broaden your behavioral choices, you have a limitless number of options. The ability to manage negative feelings and gain access to reasonable expectations while maintaining an attitude of curiosity is all that stands between you and an infinite number of possibilities. When you have the choice to be curious about and try out the possibilities presented to you in life, thoughts of "hope" and "despair" are unnecessary.

A person's beliefs provide a foundation for their behaviors. When you truly believe something, you will act in accordance with your belief. Achieving your desired outcome requires having a variety of beliefs in place. The expectation of an outcome is one type of belief. This indicates that you believe your outcome is attainable. People feel hopeless when they give up on overcoming obstacles because they don't think it's attainable, like recovering from an illness. Despair prevents people from taking the necessary steps toward recovery. Zero desired outcome expectancy means despair.

The expectation of one's own effectiveness is another type of belief. You trust that you can achieve your desired outcome and that you have the resources necessary to do it. If you believe you too have the human body's capacity to regenerate and adapt, even if you think you may need to restructure the operant mechanisms (eat differently, move differently, etc.), this is a positive indicator of your healthiness.

It's possible for an individual to believe that he or she cannot possibly achieve a desired outcome, despite the fact that he or she acknowledges that it is feasible for others to do so, such as recovering from chronic psychosomatic pain. Feelings of hopelessness are common when a person has come to the conclusion that he lacks the resources necessary to bring about his own recovery. When people lose trust, as in being certain of their own inherent capabilities, they often do nothing to improve their situation.

Both types of beliefs are necessary for individuals to take the necessary steps toward their ideal mental state. Apathy sets in when a person feels ineffective and powerless at the same time.

A person's expectation of the desired outcome and their perception of their own ability to achieve that outcome do not always line up. It's possible to have conflicting emotions about something: hope that one day you'll get what you want, and a nagging doubt that you're doomed to fail no matter what you do. Just look at the number of people who fail to keep their New Year's resolutions a few weeks after making them.

Furthermore, the converse is also obvious. You could firmly believe you have the capabilities to achieve a specific desired outcome, and then go out into the world with all your might, only to crumble when the first sign of resistance appears, making your expectation of meeting that target unrealistic in the time frame you've set. That may help to clarify why some people repeatedly go on different diets only to gain and lose the same amount of weight.

Beliefs are not always supported by a logical sequence of notions. They are, on the other hand, incredibly illogical. They are not meant to be factual. As we explained much earlier in the book, your subjective experience is very different from the objective reality you're in—you do not experience reality directly. Because you don't know the full scope of objective events in real time, you must form sets of beliefs about what happens. Beliefs serve as important filters for our internal and external experiences.

When a factual idea gets mixed up with a negative self-reliant expectation or a negative outcome expectation based on one-time learning or made-up scenarios, it causes even more problems. For example:

"I want to ask my boss for a raise" (desired outcome)

"I most likely make more sales than anyone else in the office, consistently, and so I deserve a raise." (self-reliant expectation)

"If an employee makes more money for the company, he deserves a raise, and I qualify for such" (outcome expectation)

If that is all there is to the thinking process, then the obvious behavioral choice is to approach the boss and simply say, "Dear Boss, I am consistently the top ranking salesman and I make you more money than other employees, and that is why I am here now, asking for a raise that will reflect the monetary value I give your company on a regular basis."

When fear of rejection is involved, there are limiting beliefs that hinder this behavioral choice, and their fuel is a notion that is perceived as a fact. For example:

"I want to ask my boss for a raise." (desired outcome)

"I make some sales, but can I even prove I deserve a raise?" (self-reliant expectation)

"My boss is known to never give a raise unless it's a top earning salesman" (a notion masked as a fact based on either prior experience or imagined scenarios)

"If my boss hears I want a raise, I'll be humiliated in front of everyone and made an example of. Who am I kidding? If he did not notice how hard I worked and had the idea to give me a raise on his own, I don't even stand a chance if I ask him. In fact, he might even fire me for being so rude!" (outcome expectation)

When written and analyzed in this manner, the illogical and senseless stream of thoughts in the second example becomes clear. When you're immersed in these cognitive dynamics, however, you don't analyze them the same way. Your mind interprets a physical sensation of unease as a threat of ridicule, so you play it safe by not taking any action at all. Putting your thoughts into words is not a superhuman act. You simply move your lips and utter sounds. But asking for something you want from someone who may reject you opens up all the possible outcomes, and if you have some crippling limiting beliefs, you don't care whether it's logical or not to avoid taking action in that moment, no matter how easy (physically) that action may be. You don't even bother trying.

Aristotle's model of deduction, also known as syllogism, is a method of logical reasoning that involves making a conclusion based on two premises. A syllogism consists of three parts: the major premise, the minor premise, and the conclusion.

The major premise is a general statement that establishes a general rule or principle. For example: "All humans are mortal."

The minor premise is a specific statement that provides an example or instance of the general rule. For example: "Socrates is a human."

The conclusion is the logical outcome of combining the major and minor premises. In this case, the conclusion would be: "Therefore, Socrates is mortal."

Aristotle's model of deduction is based on the idea that if the major and minor premises are true, then the conclusion must also be true. In other words, the conclusion follows logically from the premises.

For example:

Major premise: All mammals are warm-blooded.

Minor premise: Dogs are mammals.

Conclusion: Therefore, dogs are warm-blooded.

In this example, both the major and minor premises are true, so the conclusion must also be true.

The equation of deduction is simple and logical: A = B, and B = C; therefore, A = C.

Each "=" sign is really a presupposition. All you need is one bad presupposition, and you find yourself in a stream of negative thoughts that perpetuate ineffective behavioral choices.

For example:

Major premise: "Guys find only thin and fit girls attractive" (A = B)

Minor premise: "I am overweight" (B = C)

Conclusion: "I will never be asked out by any guy" (A = C)

As a result, this girl's behavior choices justify her limiting belief by being either eccentric and vulgar or extremely introverted and timid. Either way, the purpose is to shield her ego from potential rejection, because if any guy asks her out, in her mind, it is because he wants to laugh at her expense when she responds.

Aristotle's model of deduction is a useful tool for making logical arguments and for evaluating the soundness of arguments made by others. It can help to identify faulty logic or flawed reasoning and can be used to support or refute a given argument. Then, there is abduction.

Abduction is quite useful - it is a type of reasoning that involves making a hypothesis or an educated guess about the explanation for a given phenomenon. In abduction, the conclusion is drawn from the best available evidence, rather than from a set of predetermined premises. Abduction is often used in scientific inquiry and can involve making educated guesses about the causes of observed phenomena or about the implications of certain observations. If a detective investigates a crime and the house is locked with windows closed, he concludes that the perpetrator was a person who had access to the victim's house. In this case, the detective is making a hypothesis about the identity of the perpetrator based on the best available evidence.

Deduction and its inverse, abduction, allow us to combat limiting beliefs before they taint either our sense of independence or our outlook on the world as a whole. By providing an alternative mental pathway to follow when one's thoughts veer off in a negative direction, it broadens the range of actionable choices available when dealing with such expectations.

The formula for using abduction in this context is:

A = B, and C = D < B, therefore, (B > C) = A.

Instead of a limiting and crippling belief based on assumptions mixed with factual data, the young lady in the preceding example can use the same logic to completely change the belief itself:

"Guys find only thin and fit girls attractive" (A = B)

"I am overweight" (B = C)

"When I reach my target weight of 140lbs, guys will find me attractive" (B > C) = A

Observe how the final statement reinforces the result as inevitable and self-sufficient. "When" implies a certainty that she will reach her target weight, and given the preceding two premises, the only possible outcome is that guys will find her attractive at that moment. Her behavioral choices change as a result, both now and in the future. She chooses to eat healthier, exercise more, and generally care for her health. She loses weight, and this becomes the fulfillment of a self-prophecy because her mood and attitude are positive, and given that people are drawn to such energy, she becomes attractive to guys, just as she predicted.

Scan your answers throughout this book for deductive reasoning statements you've made. Look for lack of self-reliance and negative outcome expectancy types of beliefs in particular. Create a list of them in the box below. Then, using the preceding examples as guides, choose one with which you anticipate future encounters and complete the forms on the following two pages. Take note of how it affects you mentally and emotionally. So that this way of thinking sticks with you and becomes second nature, practice it as often as necessary.

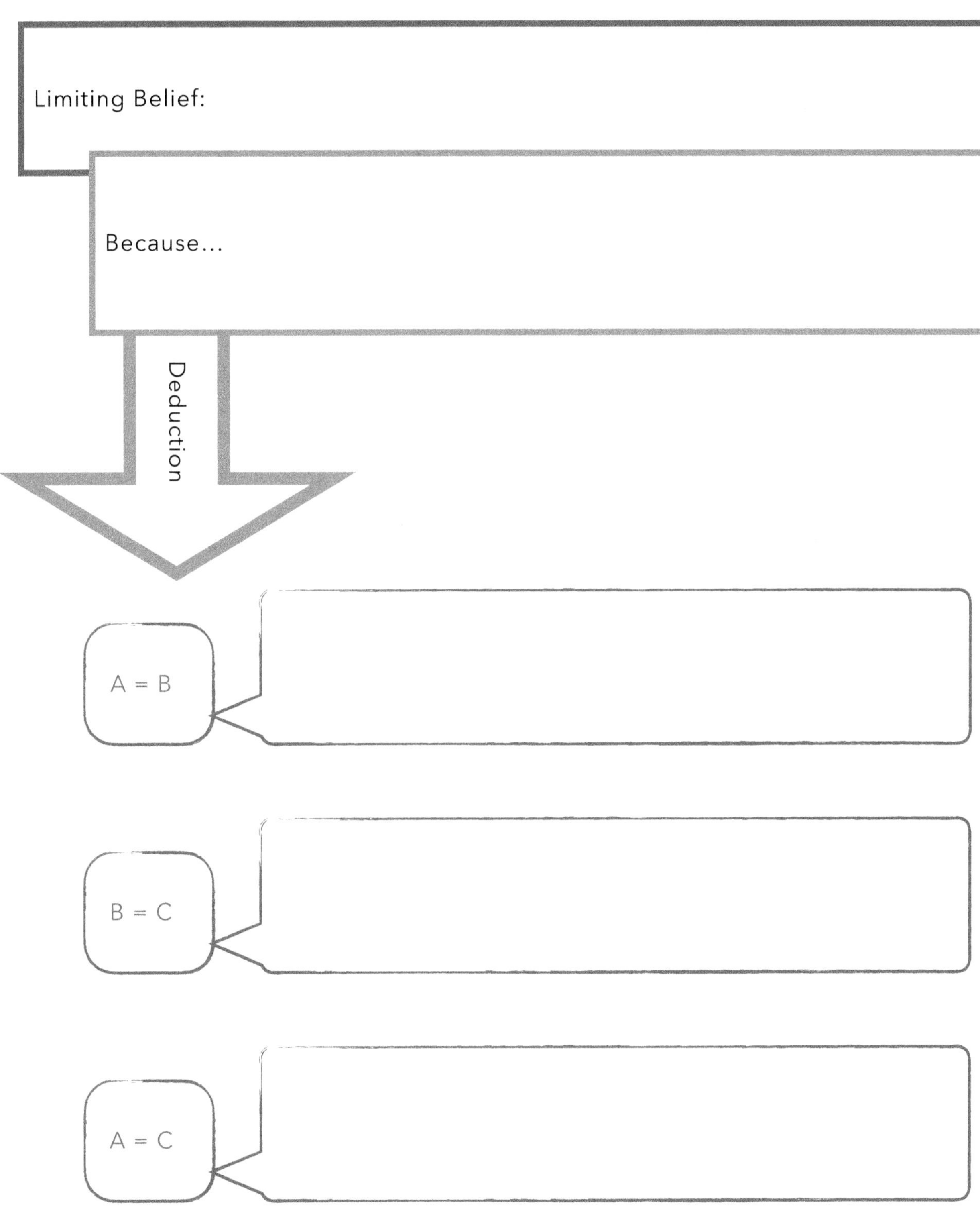

Limiting Belief:
Because...
Deduction
A = B
B = C
A = C

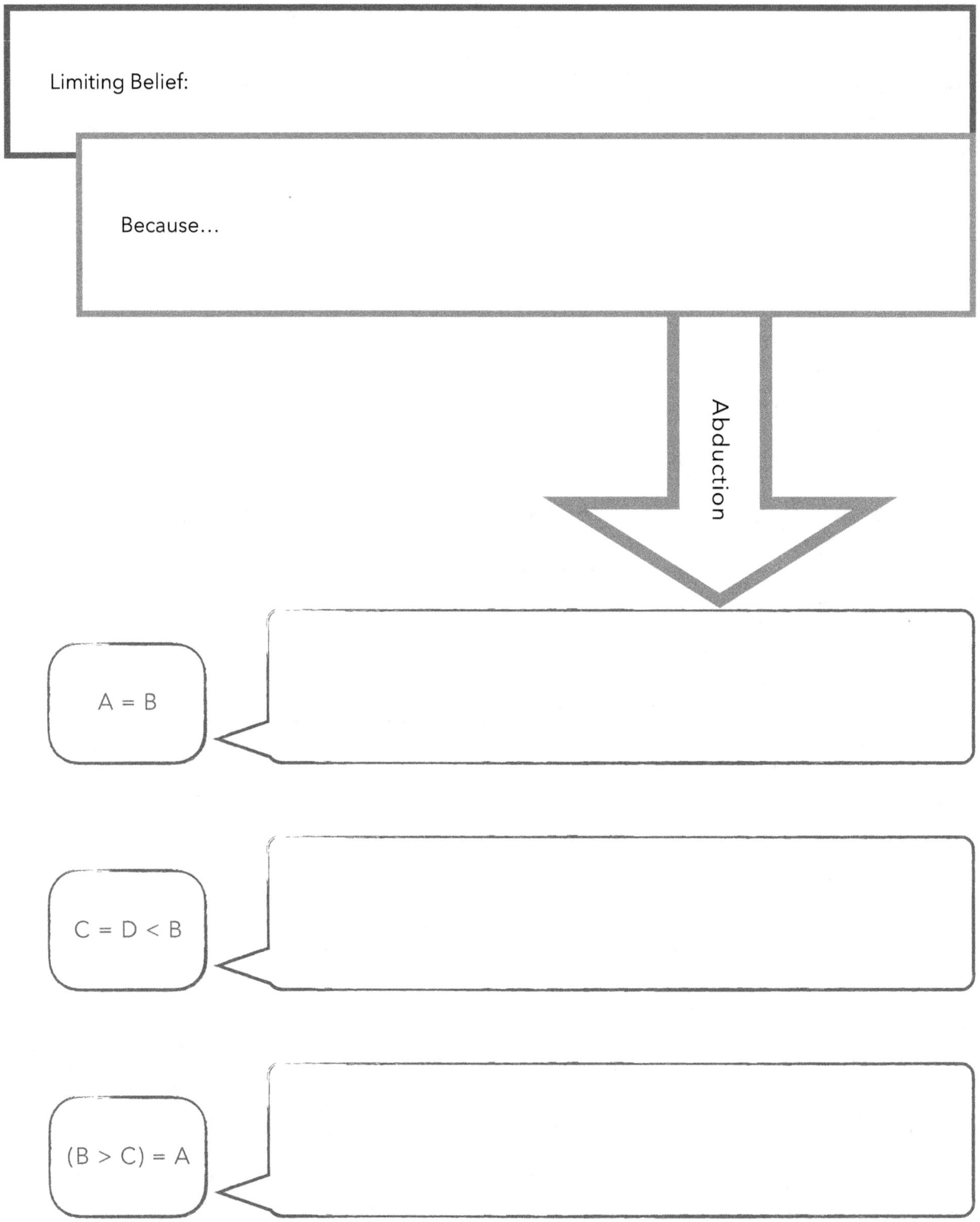

Limiting Belief:

Because...

Abduction

A = B

C = D < B

(B > C) = A

"I'm Not Good Enough"

Confirmation bias is the propensity to look for and give more weight to evidence that supports one's preexisting opinions or assumptions. Evidence that contradicts a self-deprecating belief, like a fear of being rejected may be overlooked or discounted in favor of more comforting and biased assumptions confirming data. As a result, we may start to withdraw from any interaction or situation where we might feel rejected, which can feed into the vicious cycle of anxiety and avoidance.

Nobody is going to arrest you if when cold calling a potential client, the person on the other line got angry and hung up the phone on you. You're not going to lose all of your friends and be outcasted just because a cute girl refused to go out with you. You will not lose an actual arm or a leg just because you mumbled the wrong expense figures in your presentation to the company's board of directors.

When you cold call a potential client, you're not asking for favors - it is first and foremost in the potential client's benefit to hear you out, because you are a decent salesman and you want to offer the best product for the best price in the market, and you honestly desire to give that person the best possible personal customer service. So, who benefits from you taking the lead on that scary cold call?

Asking a pretty girl out on a date is not like asking her to do you a favor. Because we live in a civilized society, you are obligated to ask a question. If you lived a hundred or more thousand years ago among cavemen and had no knowledge of language or social graces, your interaction with a beautiful woman would consist of showing her your new carved wooden knife and then grabbing her and taking her back to the cave. Thankfully, those times are over, and nowadays, if you want to get close to someone, you should make sure you're both legally and emotionally compliant. Additionally, if she accepts your proposal, she is not doing you a favor. She says yes because she is interested in learning more about you and how you can make her feel.

It's easy to see the key distinctions between the two vantage points. You are pleading for a piece of the pie with the first option, which is the one you have used thus far. With the second, however, you are the one who offers the pie. You are giving the other person a chance to take pleasure in the benefits of your existence, namely your resources both within and outside of you. Humor, friendship, a lovely singing voice, attentiveness, originality, problem-solving skills, serenity, self-confidence, and so on are all examples of your many attractive qualities. What if you lack these qualities? So prioritize them the way you see fit, and get to it! The ability to listen attentively is developed over time and is not innate. People who are great listeners must learn to be good listeners, whether intentionally or as a result of their upbringing. Our brief introduction to NLP has shown you that all human abilities are both teachable and transferable. But wait, here's the trap you're thinking about: what if they don't appreciate your piece of pie and laugh at it or throw it in your face? Even though the pie is metaphorical, it is still a humiliating experience, isn't it? As you've already learned in this book, humiliating emotions are the result of your behavioral choices, not the other person's laughter or spoken words.

Think back on the last time you felt too intimidated to even consider asking another person to "share your pie". What was the context?

What did you feel you have to offer them? What was "the pie" in that specific situation?

156

Now adopt a dissociated viewpoint, in which you observe the scene from an outsider's point of view while maintaining your sense of self in the present. Don't relive the experience; instead, watch yourself in the memory as if it were a home movie. Read the following questions aloud to yourself, and jot down the first answer that comes to mind. Asking yourself these questions out loud has two goals: to get your unconscious mind to reveal its insights and to keep your conscious mind from getting lost in the mental movie and losing touch with the outside world.

"What are some alternative explanations or perspectives that I might be overlooking?"

"What evidence do I have to support my belief, and what evidence might contradict it?"

"Are there any potential biases or prejudices that might be influencing my thinking?"

"What would I do if I had more information or a different perspective?"

"What are some potential consequences or implications of holding onto this belief?"

"What are some ways I can seek out new or diverse sources of information?"

"How might others view this situation, and what might they see that I am not considering?"

"How might this belief be holding me back or limiting my options?"

"What are some actions I can take to test or verify my belief in a more objective way?"

If none of your responses provided the insight that the only real reason you might be rejected is that the other person is genuinely uninterested in your "pie" (no matter how wonderful and delicious it may be) at that time in their life, then you must have skimmed through this book rather than working through it. If this is the case, take a week off, delete all of your answers, and start over. We warned against skipping ahead for this reason.

The bottom line is: you wrongly believe that the things you're afraid to do because you might be rejected - are not entirely about you. Nobody is doing you a favor by saying yes to what you ask of them. People say yes or no for their own personal reasons, and almost all of those reasons have nothing to do with you personally. That person either wants a piece of your pie in that moment or does not want it.

How can you embed or program that notion into your mind, so that you can start feeling good enough for being yourself, regardless of what other people may think of your pie?

It's worth thinking about the semi-revolutionary idea that you don't have to satisfy the standards (of being "good enough") of anyone, including yourself. The reason is straightforward: asking yourself, "Am I good enough?" will forever leave you feeling like you're falling short. Unless you're a narcissist, your ego will not let you be content with your current situation for more than a few minutes. Being, doing, and having more is something you will always crave. That is the human condition, and it's how our incredibly vulnerable species has managed to thrive for so long in the face of insurmountable odds. At one time, before civilization advanced and communal living became the norm, there was not a single supermarket anywhere, let alone on every corner. In order to eat, we had to go on long, exhausting expeditions of hunting, gathering, and struggling. In light of this, whenever we had the opportunity to gather more than we needed for food that day, we did so. In preparation for the coming winter, we have stockpiled food and supplies and conserved energy whenever possible. Animals don't plan ahead for the season by figuring out how much food they need to eat each day and saving some for later. We did, and because of that, we always want more. While it's true that supermarkets are now open around the clock, it will take our lizard brains several thousand more years to wire themselves for such convenience. That means it will not go away during your lifetime. Your lizard brain is never satisfied.

Rather than constantly struggling against the need to be "enough" one day, where "enough" means "more than now," we can instead try to understand the underlying structure that empowers this need and exchange it. Therefore, instead of pretending to be adequate, we eliminate the question itself from consideration. Discounting the question itself prevents the comparison circuit in the brain from being triggered.

We often compare ourselves to others and experience disappointment or frustration when we fall short because of a number of psychological and neurological factors. Social comparison theory proposes that people have a hardwired inclination to judge their own performance and that of others by drawing parallels to how they perceive those around them operating or feeling. This can be useful because it helps us learn from and get feedback from others, but it can also cause us to feel bad about ourselves if we compare ourselves to others and come to the conclusion that we are not good enough. Cultural and societal messages can also play a role by imposing unattainable standards of achievement and perfection and making it difficult to deviate from the standard. When we believe that we are falling short of these ideals, we may experience feelings of inadequacy or self-doubt.

161

On a neurobiological level, when we succeed or feel like we're making progress, the brain's reward system is activated, and this can lead to a sense of fulfillment and satisfaction. In contrast, negative emotions like frustration or disillusionment can result from a sense of falling short of our objectives or not measuring up to others.

If you're still unsure about everything you've read in this chapter, go ahead and read it again, because the antidote to the self-induced destructive virus of feeling inferior is deceptively simple. Its success, however, depends on you embedding all these lessons into your mind first. Here is the antidote:

"How can I create a mutually beneficial opportunity for that person and me through my X?"

X could mean any of the following:

Emotional intelligence: the ability to recognize and manage one's own emotions and the emotions of others.

Patience: the ability to wait calmly in the face of delays or difficulties.

Perseverance: the ability to persist in the face of challenges and setbacks.

Forgiveness: the ability to let go of grudges and resentment towards others.

Gratitude: the ability to appreciate the good things in life and express gratitude to others.

Humility: the ability to recognize one's own limitations and faults.

Compassion: the ability to feel concern for and care for others.

Courage: the ability to face challenges and adversity with bravery and determination.

Optimism: the ability to maintain a positive outlook even in difficult circumstances.

Tolerance: the ability to respect and accept the beliefs and practices of others.

Creativity: the ability to come up with new and original ideas.

Flexibility: the ability to adapt to new situations and change easily.

Honesty: the ability to be truthful and trustworthy.

Responsibility: the ability to take ownership of one's actions and fulfill obligations.

Loyalty: the ability to remain faithful and committed to others.

Respect: the ability to show consideration and regard for others.

Kindness: the ability to be considerate and caring towards others.

Fairness: the ability to treat others justly and impartially.

Generosity: the ability to give freely and selflessly to others.

Open-mindedness: the ability to be receptive to new ideas and perspectives.

While reading this list, you might have had a personal trait or skill in mind, that you hoped to see in it. Well, then, add your own in the same format (trait + description):

1.

2.

3.

4.

5.

6.

7.

8.

9.

10.

If you are having difficulty coming up with your own internal resources for whatever reason, here is a list you can use as a reference, and in the space on the right, write down random thoughts and sensations you have while desiring and considering the idea that you can nurture this attribute:

- Good-natured

- Courageous

- Conscientious

- Reliable

- Lyrical

- Knowledge

- Secure

- Attractive

- Tidy

- Non-authoritarian

- Respectful

- Brilliant

- Focused

- Extraordinary

- Deep

- Idealistic

- Patient

- Rational

- Charismatic

- Logical

- Self-sufficient

- Clever

- Efficient

- Well-read

- ▨ Punctual

- ▨ Loyal

- ▨ Helpful

- ▨ Felicific

- ▨ Forthright

- ▨ Vivacious

- ▨ Elegant

- ▨ Simple

- ▨ Hardworking

- ▨ Flexible

- ▨ Dynamic

- ▨ Prudent

- ▨ Sporting

- ▨ Intelligent

- ▨ Colorful

- ▨ Honorable

- ▨ Uncomplaining

- ▨ Esthetic

- ▨ Solid

- ▨ Stoic

- ▨ Genuine

- ▨ Individualistic

- ▨ Reverential

- ▨ Balanced

■ Freethinking

■ Tolerant

■ Invulnerable

■ Cooperative

■ Accessible

■ Considerate

■ Painstaking

■ Peaceful

■ Well-rounded

■ Methodical

■ Challenging

■ Calm

■ Skillful

■ Conciliatory

■ Enthusiastic

■ Dignified

■ Selfless

■ Providential

■ Sane

■ Firm

■ Popular

■ Amiable

■ Sage

■ Subtle

▨ Alert

▨ Observant

▨ Orderly

▨ Sympathetic

▨ Scrupulous

▨ Contemplative

▨ Sentimental

▨ Admirable

▨ Objective

▨ Suave

▨ Strong

▨ Humble

▨ Forgiving

▨ Dramatic

▨ Personable

▨ Adventurous

▨ Intuitive

▨ Forceful

▨ Clean

▨ Mature

▨ Appreciative

▨ Sensitive

▨ Aspiring

▨ Realistic

- Farsighted

- Self-reliant

- Earnest

- Impressive

- Inoffensive

- Gracious

- Gentle

- Eloquent

- Articulate

- Incisive

- Persuasive

- Teacherly

- Sexy

- Agreeable

- Wise

- Allocentric

- Understanding

- Discreet

- Creative

- Youthful

- Directed

- Principled

- Faithful

- Multi-leveled

Spontaneous

Caring

Empathetic

Optimistic

Upright

Self-denying

Clear-headed

Perfectionist

Self-defacing

Active

Precise

High-minded

Undogmatic

Trusting

Healthy

Daring

Meticulous

Open

Rustic

Benevolent

Liberal

Innovative

Debonair

Anticipative

- Dedicated

- Seraphic

- Systematic

- Well-bred

- Lovable

- Constant

- Heroic

- Generous

- Gallant

- Athletic

- Neat

- Compassionate

- Responsive

- Profound

- Curious

- Practical

- Cheerful

- Kind

- Hearty

- Exciting

- Decent

- Protective

- Organized

- Perceptive

Witty

Sharing

Patriotic

Magnanimous

Charming

Confident

Companionably

Imaginative

Sociable

Masculine or Manly

Polished

Reflective

Incorruptible

Tractable (easy to deal with)

Protean

Sophisticated

Adaptable

Shrewd

Self-critical

Romantic

Modest

Stable

Sweet

Many-sided

- ▦ Decisive

- ▦ Fair

- ▦ Capable

- ▦ Disciplined

- ▦ Studious

- ▦ Steady

- ▦ Insightful

- ▦ Dutiful

- ▦ Venturesome

- ▦ Insouciant

- ▦ Friendly

- ▦ Urbane

- ▦ Serious

- ▦ Passionate

- ▦ Honest

- ▦ Warm

- ▦ Relaxed

- ▦ Fun-loving

- ▦ Responsible

- ▦ Educated

- ▦ Moderate

- ▦ Thorough

- ▦ Ebullient

- ▦ Courteous

Playful

Original

Independent

Sober

Humorous

Scholarly

Energetic

Captivating

Cultured

A summary of your strongest qualities and attributes:

When we turn our attention away from ourselves and toward other people, we are able to reframe our perspective and concentrate on something other than our own insecurities and doubts, which can often help alleviate our fear of rejection. When we are constantly thinking about ourselves and our perceived flaws, it is easy to become consumed by a fear of rejection or the belief that we are not good enough.

This inward-looking mindset can be broken by shifting our attention to the world around us and the things that enhance and develop our desire to participate. This can help us feel more connected and engaged with the world around us, rather than isolated and disconnected. When we invest more time and energy into the efforts and interactions that make our lives more meaningful, we often experience an increase in feelings of competence and self-assurance.

Furthermore, by focusing on others, we can find greater fulfillment and meaning in our own lives. When we focus on helping others or contributing to something bigger than ourselves, we may feel more fulfilled and energized. This can boost our capacity for intuitive self-expression, making us feel more comfortable putting ourselves out there and, in turn, less vulnerable to rejection.

Finally, reversing the polarity on the direction of our attention in the present requires a deliberate behavioral choice: moving from an "outside → inside" orientation, as when evaluating oneself in relation to others, to an "inside → outside" orientation, as when drawing upon personal internal resources and generously imparting them to others for the common good.

A new daily script is provided below. Follow the same instructions as with the first script in this book.

Begin by finding a quiet and comfortable place to sit or lie down. Close your eyes and take several deep breaths, concentrating on the sensation of air flowing in and out of your body.

Imagine that your mind is like a sound system where different thoughts and feelings are played like songs. Some of these thoughts and feelings may be beneficial and positive, while others may be detrimental and negative.

As you continue to breathe deeply, imagine that you have the ability to choose which thoughts and feelings play on your mental sound system. You can choose to increase the volume of positive and beneficial thoughts while decreasing the volume of intrusive and negative thoughts.

Now recall an annoying thought that has been bothering you. Take note of how it makes you feel and the effect it has on your body.

Assume you have a dial or a volume control for this thought. Reduce the volume of this intrusive thought gradually and deliberately until it is barely audible.

Allow yourself to relax and let go of any tension or anxiety caused by the intrusive thought as the volume of it decreases.

Consider turning up the volume on a positive thought or feeling you want to focus on. This could be a sense of calm, confidence, or acceptance of oneself. Allow this positive thought or feeling to fully embrace you and fill your mind and body.

Continue to practice turning off intrusive thoughts and turning on positive thoughts and feelings whenever they arise. You will gradually improve your ability to manage your mental sound system and regulate your thoughts and emotions.

When you're ready, slowly open your eyes, feeling refreshed and in command of your thoughts.

Use the form on the next page to track your early morning dreams and insights.

Day	Date	Insights / Early Morning Dreams
1		
2		
3		
4		
5		
6		
7		
8		
9		
10		

Day	Date	Insights / Early Morning Dreams
11		
12		
13		
14		
15		
16		
17		
18		
19		
20		

Day	Date	Insights / Early Morning Dreams
21		
22		
23		
24		
25		
26		
27		
28		
29		
30		

Bibliography

An Insiders Guide to Sub Modalities, Will Macdonald and Richard Bandler, 1989

An Introduction to NLP Neuro-Linguistic Programming : Psychological Skills for Understanding and Influencing People, Joseph O'Connor, 1998

Awaken the Giant Within : How to Take Immediate Control of Your Mental, Emotional, Physical and Financial Destiny!, Anthony Robbins, 1992

Beliefs: Pathways to Health and Wellbeing, Robert Dilts, Tim Hallbom, and Suzi Smith, 1990

Blink: The Power of Thinking Without Thinking: Gladwell, M. (2005). Little, Brown and Company.

Changing Belief Systems With NLP, Robert Dilts, 1990

Change Your Mind-And Keep the Change : Advanced NLP Sub-modalities Interventions, Connirae Andreas, Steve Andreas, Michael Eric Bennett, and Donna Wilson, 1987

Dynamic Learning, Robert B. Dilts and Todd A. Epstein, 1995

Encyclopedia of Systemic Neuro-Linguistic Programming and NLP New Coding, Robert B. Dilts and Judith A. Delozier, 2000

Frogs into Princes: Neuro Linguistic Programming, Richard Bandler, John Grinder, Steve Andreas, and John O. Srevens, 1979

From Coach to Awakener, Robert Dilts, 2003

Get the Life You Want: The Secrets to Quick and Lasting Life Change with Neuro-Linguistic Programming, Richard Bandler, 2008

Giant Steps : Author Of Awaken The Giant And Unlimited Power, Anthony Robbins, 1997

Heart of the Mind: Engaging Your Inner Power to Change with Neuro-Linguistic Programming, Connirae Andreas and Steve Andreas, 1989

Jay Haley On Milton H. Erickson, Jay Haley, 1993

Magic In Action, Richard Bandler, 1982

Mindworks: An Introduction to Nlp: the Secrets of Your Mind Revealed, Anne Linden, 1998

Manage Yourself, Manage Your Life: Vital Nlp Techniques for Personal Well-Being and Professional Success, Ian McDermott and Ian Shircore, 1999

Modeling With NLP, Robert Dilts, 1998

My Voice Will Go With You: The Teaching Tales of Milton H. Erickson, M.D., Sidney Rosen, 1991

Neuro-Linguistic Programming: Volume I (The Study of the Structure of Subjective Experience), Robert Dilts, 1980

NLP at Work, Second Edition: How to Model What Works in Business to Make It Work for You (People Skills for Professionals), Sue Knight, 2002

NLP: The New Technology Of Achievement, NLP Comprehensive, Charles Faulkner and Steve Andreas, 1996

NLP Workbook: A Practical Guide to Achieving the Results You Want, Joseph O'Connor, 2001

Obedience to Authority: Milgram, S. (1974). Harper & Row.

Patterns of the Hypnotic Techniques of Milton H. Erickson, M.D. (Volume I), Richard; Grinder, John Bandler, 1975

Patterns of the Hypnotic Techniques of Milton H. Erickson, M.D., Vol. 2, John Grinder, Judith Delozier, and Richard Bandler, 1997

Persuasion Engineering, Richard Bandler and John LA Valle, 1996

Presenting Magically: Transforming Your Stage Presence with NLP, Tad James and David Shephard, 2001

Personality Selling : Using NLP and the Enneagram to Understand People and How They Are Influenced, Albert J. Valentino, 1999

Precision: A New Approach to Communication : How to Get the Information You Need to Get Results, Michael McMaster and John Grinder, 1993

Reframing: Neuro-linguistic Programming and The Transformation of Meaning, Richard Bandler and John Grinder, 1982

Roots Of Neuro Linguistic Programming, Robert Dilts, 1983

Skills for the Future: Managing Creativity and Innovation, Robert Dilts and Gino Bonissone, 1993

Sleight Of Mouth: The Magic Of Conversational Belief Change, Robert Dilts, 2006

Sourcebook of Magic: A Comprehensive Guide to NLP Change Patterns, Michael L. Hall and Barbara P. Belnap, 2001

Strategies of Genius, Volume One, Robert Dilts, 1994

Strategies of Genius, Volume Two, Robert Dilts, 1994

Successful Selling With NLP: Powerful Ways to Help You Connect with Customers, Joseph O'Connor, 2001

Success Mastery With NLP/Cassettes, Charles Faulkner, 1994

The Emotional Life of Your Brain: Davidson, R.J., & Begley, S. (2012). Plume.

The Enneagram and NLP: A Journey of Evolution, Anne Linden and Murray Spalding, 1994

The Lucifer Effect: Understanding How Good People Turn Evil: Zimbardo, P. (2007). Random House.

The power of compassion, Dalai Lama, New York: HarperCollins, 1995

The Selfish Gene: Dawkins, R. (1976). Oxford University Press.

The Social Psychology of Good and Evil: Markman, A. (2013). Guilford Press.

The Spirit Of NLP, L. Michael Hall, 2001

The Structure of Magic: A Book About Language and Therapy (Structure of Magic), Richard Bandler and John Grinder, 1975

The Structure of Magic II: A Book About Language and Therapy (Book 2), Richard Bandler and John Grinder, 1975

The Theory of Cognitive Dissonance: Aronson, E. (1972). Stanford University Press.

The Tipping Point: How Little Things Can Make a Big Difference. Gladwell, M. (2000). Little, Brown and Company.

The Wisdom of Milton H. Erickson: The Complete Volume, Ronald A. Havens, 2005

The Unbearable Lightness of Being: Kundera, M. (1984). Harper & Row.

Thinking, Fast and Slow: Kahneman, D. (2011) Farrar, Straus and Giroux

Tools of the Spirit, Robert Dilts and Robert McDonald, 1997

Training With NLP, Joseph O'Connor, 1994

Training Trances: Multi-Level Communication in Therapy and Training, John Overdurf and Julie Silverthorn, 1995

Trance-Formations: Neuro-Linguistic Programming and the Structure of Hypnosis, John Grinder and Richard Bandler, 1981

Transforming Your Self: Becoming Who You Want to Be, Steve Andreas, 2002

Turtles All the Way Down: Prerequisites to Personal Genius, John Grinder and Judith Delozier, 1995

Uncommon Therapy: The Psychiatric Techniques of Milton H. Erickson, M.D., Jay Haley, 1993

Unlimited Power : The New Science Of Personal Achievement, Anthony Robbins, 1997

User's Manual for the Brain, Vol. II: Mastering Systemic NLP, L. Michael Hall and Bob G. Bodenhamer, 2003

Using Your Brain—For a Change: Neuro-Linguistic Programming, Richard Bandler, 1985

Virginia Satir: the Patterns of Her Magic, Steve Andreas, 1999

Visionary Leadership Skills: Creating a World to Which People Want to Belong, RobertB.Dilts,1996

Forms & Templates

Experience	Age / Year	Event Title
A		
B		
C		
D		
E		
F		
G		

Experience	Age / Year	Event Title
A		
B		
C		
D		
E		
F		
G		

Experience	Age / Year	Event Title
A		
B		
C		
D		
E		
F		
G		

Epoch __

Experience	Age / Year	Event Title
A		
B		
C		
D		
E		
F		
G		

Date & Time:

Context:

People Involved:

Event (A Brief Objective Description):

Actual Behavioral Choices (Thoughts, Actions):

Alternative Behavioral Choices:

Eventual Outcome:

Potential Outcome:

Date & Time: Context:

People Involved:

Event (A Brief Objective Description):

Actual Behavioral Choices (Thoughts, Actions):	Alternative Behavioral Choices:
Eventual Outcome:	Potential Outcome:

Expansion of Available Behavioral Choices

Date & Time: Context:

People Involved:

Event (A Brief Objective Description):

| Actual Behavioral Choices (Thoughts, Actions): | Alternative Behavioral Choices: |

Eventual Outcome: Potential Outcome:

Expansion of Available Behavioral Choices

Date & Time: Context:

People Involved:

Event (A Brief Objective Description):

Actual Behavioral Choices (Thoughts, Actions):   Alternative Behavioral Choices:

Eventual Outcome: Potential Outcome:

Day	Date	Insights / Early Morning Dreams
1		
2		
3		
4		
5		
6		
7		
8		
9		
10		

Day	Date	Insights / Early Morning Dreams
11		
12		
13		
14		
15		
16		
17		
18		
19		
20		

Day	Date	Insights / Early Morning Dreams
21		
22		
23		
24		
25		
26		
27		
28		
29		
30		

<table>
<thead>
<tr><th>Day</th><th>Date</th><th>Insights / Early Morning Dreams</th></tr>
</thead>
<tbody>
<tr><td>1</td><td></td><td></td></tr>
<tr><td>2</td><td></td><td></td></tr>
<tr><td>3</td><td></td><td></td></tr>
<tr><td>4</td><td></td><td></td></tr>
<tr><td>5</td><td></td><td></td></tr>
<tr><td>6</td><td></td><td></td></tr>
<tr><td>7</td><td></td><td></td></tr>
<tr><td>8</td><td></td><td></td></tr>
<tr><td>9</td><td></td><td></td></tr>
<tr><td>10</td><td></td><td></td></tr>
</tbody>
</table>

Day	Date	Insights / Early Morning Dreams
11		
12		
13		
14		
15		
16		
17		
18		
19		
20		

Day	Date	Insights / Early Morning Dreams
21		
22		
23		
24		
25		
26		
27		
28		
29		
30		

Memory (title):

Visual Sub-modalities Elicitation   Intensity

▷ Movie   ▷ Still Image   ① ② ③ ④ ⑤ ⑥ ⑦ ⑧ ⑨

▷ Associated   ▷ Dissociated   ① ② ③ ④ ⑤ ⑥ ⑦ ⑧ ⑨

▷ Color   ▷ Black & White   ① ② ③ ④ ⑤ ⑥ ⑦ ⑧ ⑨

▷ Location: ↑ → ↓ ←   ① ② ③ ④ ⑤ ⑥ ⑦ ⑧ ⑨

▷ Distance: Close   ▷ Distance: Far   ① ② ③ ④ ⑤ ⑥ ⑦ ⑧ ⑨

▷ Light: Dim   ▷ Light: Bright   ① ② ③ ④ ⑤ ⑥ ⑦ ⑧ ⑨

▷ Contrast: Vibrant   ▷ Contrast: Damp   ① ② ③ ④ ⑤ ⑥ ⑦ ⑧ ⑨

▷ Size: Small   ▷ Size: Large   ① ② ③ ④ ⑤ ⑥ ⑦ ⑧ ⑨

▷ Focus: Sharp   ▷ Focus: Blurr   ① ② ③ ④ ⑤ ⑥ ⑦ ⑧ ⑨

▷ Speed: Slow   ▷ Speed: Fast   ① ② ③ ④ ⑤ ⑥ ⑦ ⑧ ⑨

▷ Panoramic   ▷ Framed   ① ② ③ ④ ⑤ ⑥ ⑦ ⑧ ⑨

▷ Texture: Smooth   ▷ Texture: Rough   ① ② ③ ④ ⑤ ⑥ ⑦ ⑧ ⑨

▷ Dimension: 3D   ▷ Flat   ① ② ③ ④ ⑤ ⑥ ⑦ ⑧ ⑨

Memory (title):

Visual Sub-modalities Elicitation   Intensity

▷ Movie   ▷ Still Image   ① ② ③ ④ ⑤ ⑥ ⑦ ⑧ ⑨

▷ Associated   ▷ Dissociated   ① ② ③ ④ ⑤ ⑥ ⑦ ⑧ ⑨

▷ Color   ▷ Black & White   ① ② ③ ④ ⑤ ⑥ ⑦ ⑧ ⑨

▷ Location: ↑ → ↓ ←   ① ② ③ ④ ⑤ ⑥ ⑦ ⑧ ⑨

▷ Distance: Close ▷ Distance: Far   ① ② ③ ④ ⑤ ⑥ ⑦ ⑧ ⑨

▷ Light: Dim   ▷ Light: Bright   ① ② ③ ④ ⑤ ⑥ ⑦ ⑧ ⑨

▷ Contrast: Vibrant ▷ Contrast: Damp ① ② ③ ④ ⑤ ⑥ ⑦ ⑧ ⑨

▷ Size: Small   ▷ Size: Large   ① ② ③ ④ ⑤ ⑥ ⑦ ⑧ ⑨

▷ Focus: Sharp   ▷ Focus: Blurr   ① ② ③ ④ ⑤ ⑥ ⑦ ⑧ ⑨

▷ Speed: Slow   ▷ Speed: Fast   ① ② ③ ④ ⑤ ⑥ ⑦ ⑧ ⑨

▷ Panoramic   ▷ Framed   ① ② ③ ④ ⑤ ⑥ ⑦ ⑧ ⑨

▷ Texture: Smooth ▷ Texture: Rough   ① ② ③ ④ ⑤ ⑥ ⑦ ⑧ ⑨

▷ Dimension: 3D   ▷ Flat   ① ② ③ ④ ⑤ ⑥ ⑦ ⑧ ⑨

Visual Sub-modalities Elicitation   Intensity

▷ Movie   ▷ Still Image   ① ② ③ ④ ⑤ ⑥ ⑦ ⑧ ⑨

▷ Associated   ▷ Dissociated   ① ② ③ ④ ⑤ ⑥ ⑦ ⑧ ⑨

▷ Color   ▷ Black & White   ① ② ③ ④ ⑤ ⑥ ⑦ ⑧ ⑨

▷ Location: ↑ → ↓ ←   ① ② ③ ④ ⑤ ⑥ ⑦ ⑧ ⑨

▷ Distance: Close ▷ Distance: Far   ① ② ③ ④ ⑤ ⑥ ⑦ ⑧ ⑨

▷ Light: Dim   ▷ Light: Bright   ① ② ③ ④ ⑤ ⑥ ⑦ ⑧ ⑨

▷ Contrast: Vibrant ▷ Contrast: Damp   ① ② ③ ④ ⑤ ⑥ ⑦ ⑧ ⑨

▷ Size: Small   ▷ Size: Large   ① ② ③ ④ ⑤ ⑥ ⑦ ⑧ ⑨

▷ Focus: Sharp   ▷ Focus: Blurr   ① ② ③ ④ ⑤ ⑥ ⑦ ⑧ ⑨

▷ Speed: Slow   ▷ Speed: Fast   ① ② ③ ④ ⑤ ⑥ ⑦ ⑧ ⑨

▷ Panoramic   ▷ Framed   ① ② ③ ④ ⑤ ⑥ ⑦ ⑧ ⑨

▷ Texture: Smooth ▷ Texture: Rough   ① ② ③ ④ ⑤ ⑥ ⑦ ⑧ ⑨

▷ Dimension: 3D   ▷ Flat   ① ② ③ ④ ⑤ ⑥ ⑦ ⑧ ⑨

Memory (title):

Visual Sub-modalities Elicitation   Intensity

▷ Movie   ▷ Still Image   ① ② ③ ④ ⑤ ⑥ ⑦ ⑧ ⑨

▷ Associated   ▷ Dissociated   ① ② ③ ④ ⑤ ⑥ ⑦ ⑧ ⑨

▷ Color   ▷ Black & White   ① ② ③ ④ ⑤ ⑥ ⑦ ⑧ ⑨

▷ Location: ↑ → ↓ ←   ① ② ③ ④ ⑤ ⑥ ⑦ ⑧ ⑨

▷ Distance: Close   ▷ Distance: Far   ① ② ③ ④ ⑤ ⑥ ⑦ ⑧ ⑨

▷ Light: Dim   ▷ Light: Bright   ① ② ③ ④ ⑤ ⑥ ⑦ ⑧ ⑨

▷ Contrast: Vibrant ▷ Contrast: Damp   ① ② ③ ④ ⑤ ⑥ ⑦ ⑧ ⑨

▷ Size: Small   ▷ Size: Large   ① ② ③ ④ ⑤ ⑥ ⑦ ⑧ ⑨

▷ Focus: Sharp   ▷ Focus: Blurr   ① ② ③ ④ ⑤ ⑥ ⑦ ⑧ ⑨

▷ Speed: Slow   ▷ Speed: Fast   ① ② ③ ④ ⑤ ⑥ ⑦ ⑧ ⑨

▷ Panoramic   ▷ Framed   ① ② ③ ④ ⑤ ⑥ ⑦ ⑧ ⑨

▷ Texture: Smooth   ▷ Texture: Rough   ① ② ③ ④ ⑤ ⑥ ⑦ ⑧ ⑨

▷ Dimension: 3D   ▷ Flat   ① ② ③ ④ ⑤ ⑥ ⑦ ⑧ ⑨

Memory (title):

Auditory Sub-modalities Elicitation   Intensity

▷ Self-Talk: Own   ▷ Self-Talk: Other   ① ② ③ ④ ⑤ ⑥ ⑦ ⑧ ⑨
   Voice   Voice

▷ Pitch: Low   ▷ Pitch: High   ① ② ③ ④ ⑤ ⑥ ⑦ ⑧ ⑨

▷ Content   ▷ Syntax / Form   ① ② ③ ④ ⑤ ⑥ ⑦ ⑧ ⑨

▷ Emotional Expression   ① ② ③ ④ ⑤ ⑥ ⑦ ⑧ ⑨

▷ Volume: Low   ▷ Volume: High   ① ② ③ ④ ⑤ ⑥ ⑦ ⑧ ⑨

▷ Harmonic   ▷ Disharmonic   ① ② ③ ④ ⑤ ⑥ ⑦ ⑧ ⑨

▷ Tempo: Fast   ▷ Tempo: Slow   ① ② ③ ④ ⑤ ⑥ ⑦ ⑧ ⑨

▷ Location In Space: ① ② ③ ④ ⑤ ⑥ ⑦ ⑧ ⑨

▷ Monotonic   ▷ Inflections   ① ② ③ ④ ⑤ ⑥ ⑦ ⑧ ⑨

▷ Long Speech   ▷ Short Bursts   ① ② ③ ④ ⑤ ⑥ ⑦ ⑧ ⑨

▷ Key Words (digital):   ① ② ③ ④ ⑤ ⑥ ⑦ ⑧ ⑨

Memory (title):

Auditory Sub-modalities Elicitation   Intensity

▷ Self-Talk: Own   ▷ Self-Talk: Other   ① ② ③ ④ ⑤ ⑥ ⑦ ⑧ ⑨
  Voice   Voice

▷ Pitch: Low   ▷ Pitch: High   ① ② ③ ④ ⑤ ⑥ ⑦ ⑧ ⑨

▷ Content   ▷ Syntax / Form   ① ② ③ ④ ⑤ ⑥ ⑦ ⑧ ⑨

▷ Emotional Expression   ① ② ③ ④ ⑤ ⑥ ⑦ ⑧ ⑨

▷ Volume: Low   ▷ Volume: High   ① ② ③ ④ ⑤ ⑥ ⑦ ⑧ ⑨

▷ Harmonic   ▷ Disharmonic   ① ② ③ ④ ⑤ ⑥ ⑦ ⑧ ⑨

▷ Tempo: Fast   ▷ Tempo: Slow   ① ② ③ ④ ⑤ ⑥ ⑦ ⑧ ⑨

▷ Location In Space: ① ② ③ ④ ⑤ ⑥ ⑦ ⑧ ⑨

▷ Monotonic   ▷ Inflections   ① ② ③ ④ ⑤ ⑥ ⑦ ⑧ ⑨

▷ Long Speech   ▷ Short Bursts   ① ② ③ ④ ⑤ ⑥ ⑦ ⑧ ⑨

▷ Key Words (digital):   ① ② ③ ④ ⑤ ⑥ ⑦ ⑧ ⑨

Memory (title):

Auditory Sub-modalities Elicitation   Intensity

▷ Self-Talk: Own Voice   ▷ Self-Talk: Other Voice   ① ② ③ ④ ⑤ ⑥ ⑦ ⑧ ⑨

▷ Pitch: Low   ▷ Pitch: High   ① ② ③ ④ ⑤ ⑥ ⑦ ⑧ ⑨

▷ Content   ▷ Syntax / Form   ① ② ③ ④ ⑤ ⑥ ⑦ ⑧ ⑨

▷ Emotional Expression   ① ② ③ ④ ⑤ ⑥ ⑦ ⑧ ⑨

▷ Volume: Low   ▷ Volume: High   ① ② ③ ④ ⑤ ⑥ ⑦ ⑧ ⑨

▷ Harmonic   ▷ Disharmonic   ① ② ③ ④ ⑤ ⑥ ⑦ ⑧ ⑨

▷ Tempo: Fast   ▷ Tempo: Slow   ① ② ③ ④ ⑤ ⑥ ⑦ ⑧ ⑨

▷ Location In Space: ① ② ③ ④ ⑤ ⑥ ⑦ ⑧ ⑨

▷ Monotonic   ▷ Inflections   ① ② ③ ④ ⑤ ⑥ ⑦ ⑧ ⑨

▷ Long Speech   ▷ Short Bursts   ① ② ③ ④ ⑤ ⑥ ⑦ ⑧ ⑨

▷ Key Words (digital):   ① ② ③ ④ ⑤ ⑥ ⑦ ⑧ ⑨

Memory (title):

Auditory Sub-modalities Elicitation   Intensity

▷ Self-Talk: Own   ▷ Self-Talk: Other   ① ② ③ ④ ⑤ ⑥ ⑦ ⑧ ⑨
  Voice   Voice

▷ Pitch: Low   ▷ Pitch: High   ① ② ③ ④ ⑤ ⑥ ⑦ ⑧ ⑨

▷ Content   ▷ Syntax / Form   ① ② ③ ④ ⑤ ⑥ ⑦ ⑧ ⑨

▷ Emotional Expression   ① ② ③ ④ ⑤ ⑥ ⑦ ⑧ ⑨

▷ Volume: Low   ▷ Volume: High   ① ② ③ ④ ⑤ ⑥ ⑦ ⑧ ⑨

▷ Harmonic   ▷ Disharmonic   ① ② ③ ④ ⑤ ⑥ ⑦ ⑧ ⑨

▷ Tempo: Fast   ▷ Tempo: Slow   ① ② ③ ④ ⑤ ⑥ ⑦ ⑧ ⑨

▷ Location In Space: ① ② ③ ④ ⑤ ⑥ ⑦ ⑧ ⑨

▷ Monotonic   ▷ Inflections   ① ② ③ ④ ⑤ ⑥ ⑦ ⑧ ⑨

▷ Long Speech   ▷ Short Bursts   ① ② ③ ④ ⑤ ⑥ ⑦ ⑧ ⑨

▷ Key Words (digital):   ① ② ③ ④ ⑤ ⑥ ⑦ ⑧ ⑨

Day / Time	I Felt / Thought...	Perhaps because of...

Day / Time	I Felt / Thought...	Perhaps because of...

Day / Time	I Felt / Thought...	Perhaps because of...

Day / Time	I Felt / Thought...	Perhaps because of...

What would happen if you did?

What would not happen if you did?

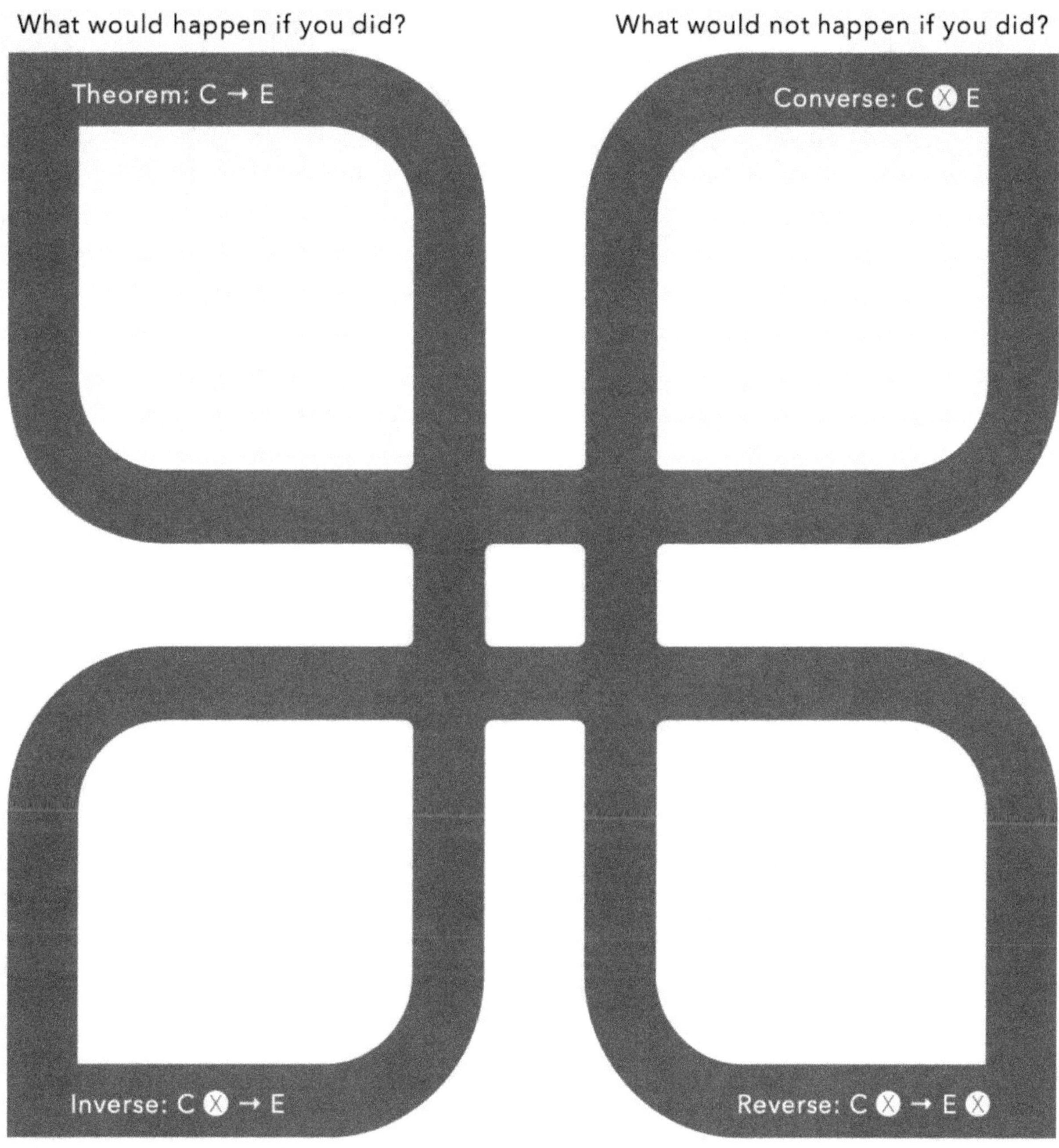

What would happen if you did not?

What would not happen if you did not?

* C=cause
* E=Event

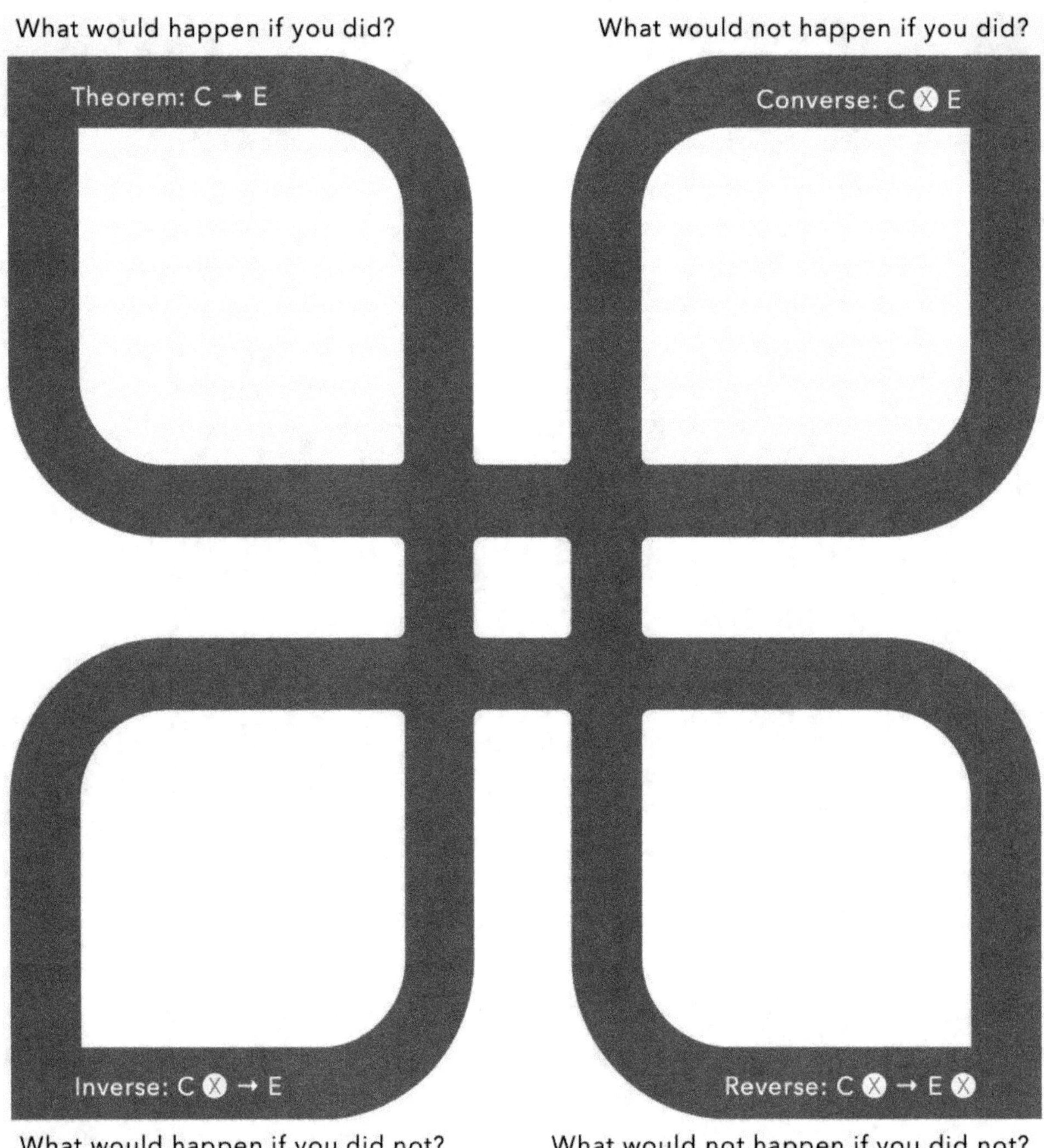

* C=cause
* E=Event

What would happen if you did?   What would not happen if you did?

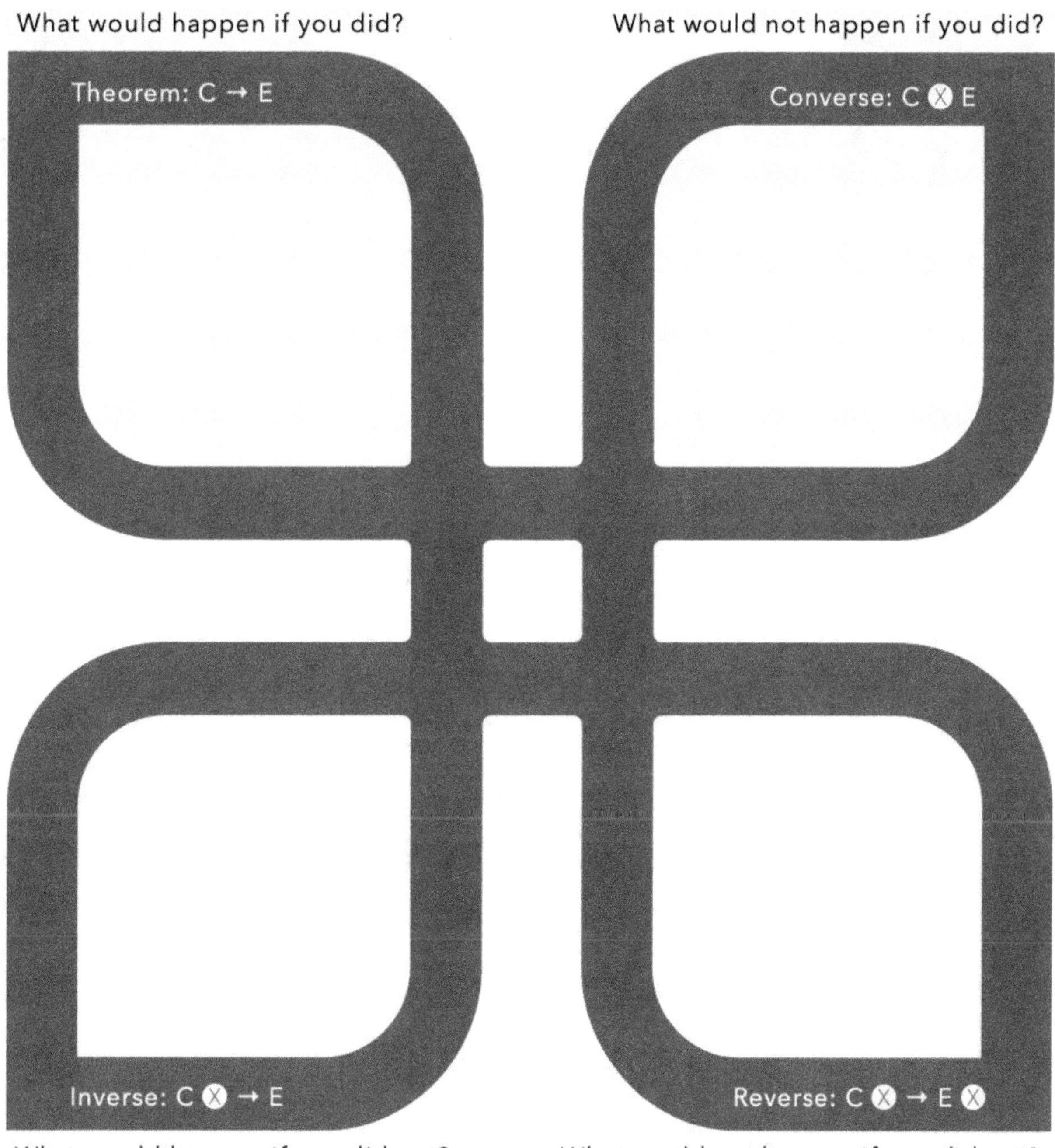

What would happen if you did not?   What would not happen if you did not?

* C=cause
* E=Event

What would happen if you did?   What would not happen if you did?

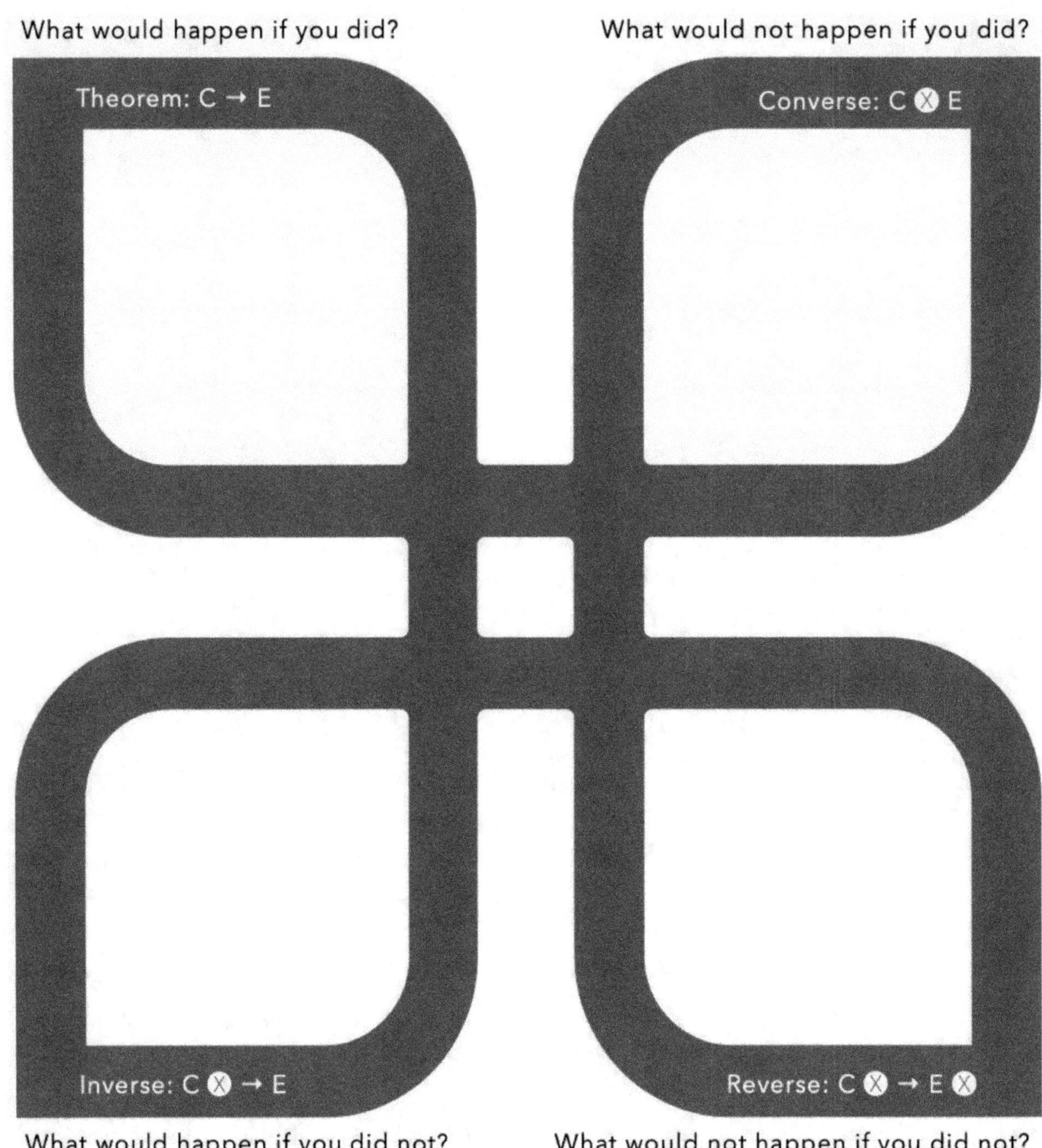

What would happen if you did not?   What would not happen if you did not?

* C=cause
* E=Event

Limiting Belief:

Because...

Deduction

A = B

B = C

A = C

Limiting Belief:

Because…

Abduction

A = B

C = D < B

(B > C) = A

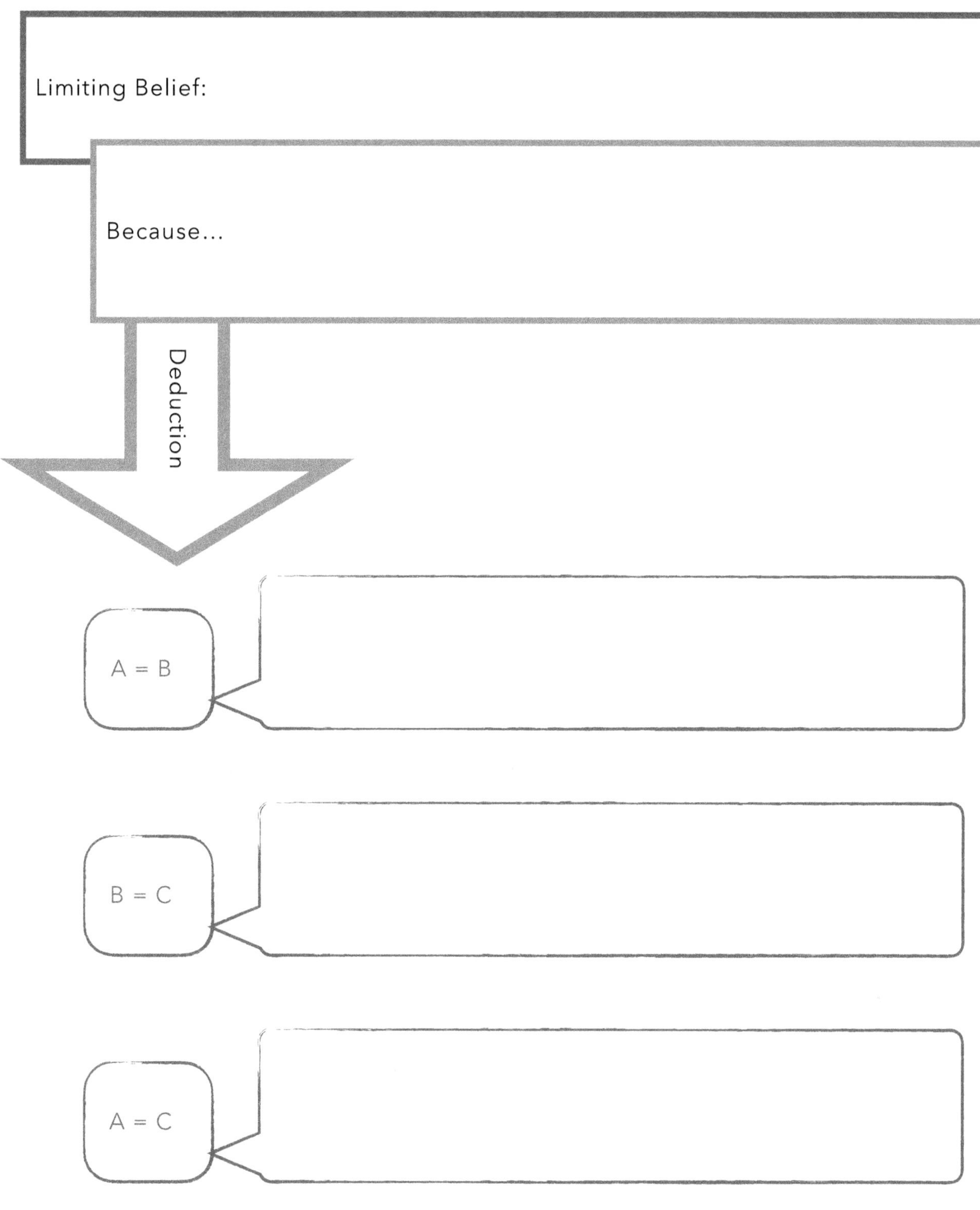

Limiting Belief:
Because...
Deduction
A = B
B = C
A = C

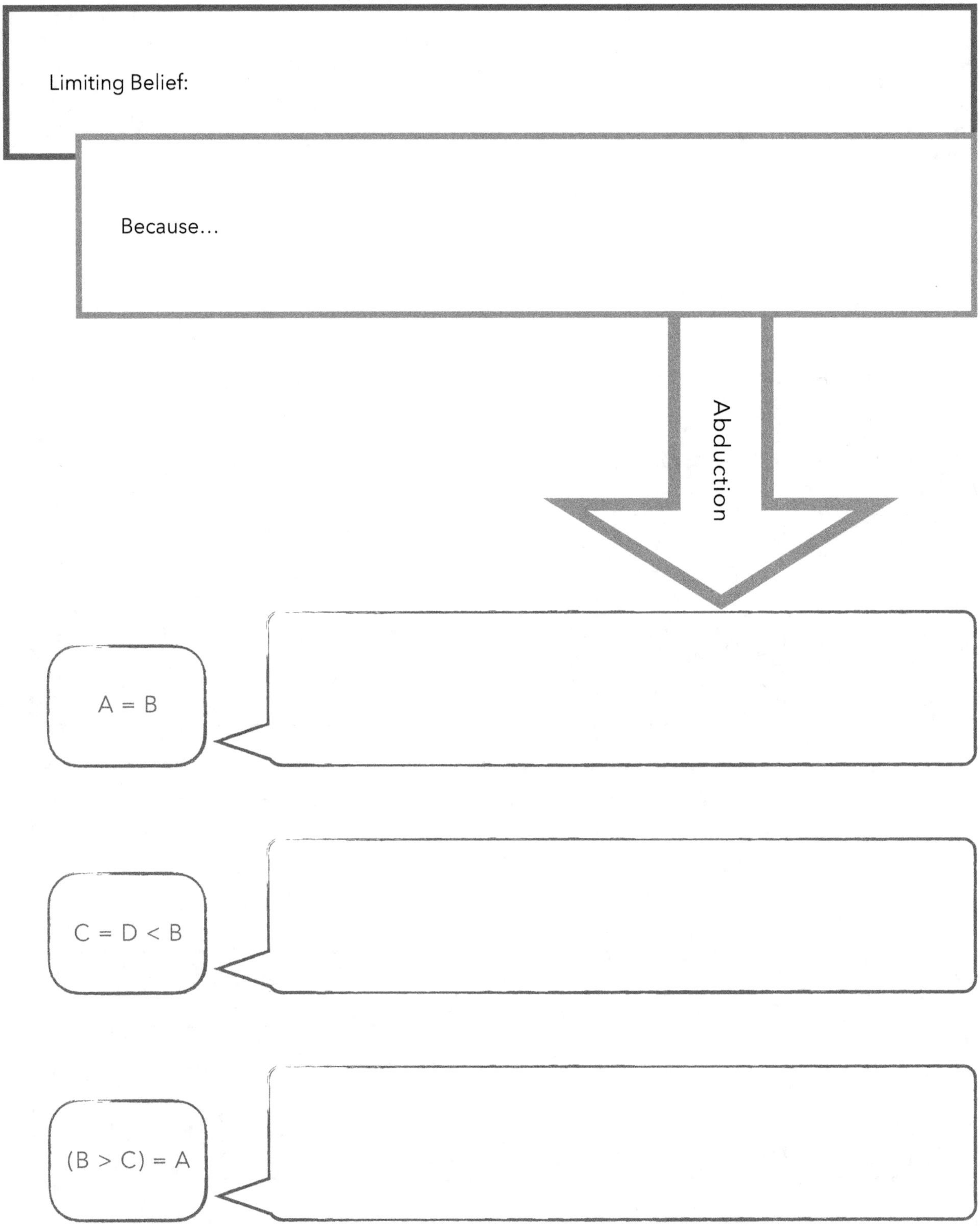

Limiting Belief:

Because...

Abduction

A = B

C = D < B

(B > C) = A

A friendly reminder:

$$\text{Subjective Experience} = \text{Event} + \text{Reaction}$$

Your Life Is Not on Hold

Milton Erickson said: *"Life isn't something you can give an answer to today. You should enjoy the process of waiting, the process of becoming what you are. There is nothing more delightful than planting flower seeds and not knowing what kind of flowers are going to come up."*

As you come to the end of this book, we hope that you feel excited and motivated to keep working on yourself and making positive changes in your life. Remember, personal growth and self-improvement are ongoing processes, and it is important to continue learning and applying what you have learned in your daily life.

One of the most important things you can do for yourself is to become curious about life and seize opportunities with excitement to see what happens. Don't be afraid to step outside of your comfort zone and try new things - this is where the magic of personal growth and self-improvement truly lies.

While it may be easy to get discouraged or lose motivation at times, it is important to remind yourself of the progress you have already made and the positive changes that have resulted from your efforts. Take a moment to reflect on all that you have learned and accomplished so far, and let this serve as a source of inspiration and motivation to keep going. As you continue on your journey of self-improvement, don't be too hard on yourself. Remember, progress is not always a straight line - there will be setbacks and challenges along the way. The important thing is to keep moving forward, learning from your mistakes, and continuing to strive for excellence in all aspects of your life.

We encourage you to take the time to review and practice the strategies and techniques that you have learned throughout this book. It is through repetition and practice that we truly internalize and make lasting changes in our lives. We wish you all the best on your journey of personal growth and self-improvement. May you find success and fulfillment in all that you do, and may you continue to strive for excellence in all aspects of your life. Remember, with hard work and determination, anything is possible. And don't forget to have fun and enjoy the journey - after all, life is meant to be lived to the fullest!

If you have any questions or comments, or you're in need for a personal advice - we'd love to hear from you. Contact us at
www.ericks.org